Praise for *Named for Glory*

"The Trinity is a communion of eternal love between the Father and the Son in the unity of the Holy Spirit. St. Elizabeth of the Trinity can help us discover that we are a holy temple where God is always present, thanks to the grace of Baptism. This book shows us how to open our hearts to this mystery of the Trinity and how to be sanctified and transformed by grace."

— ***Cardinal Anders Arborelius, O.C.D.,***
Bishop, Diocese of Stockholm, Sweden

"Since St. Elizabeth of the Trinity's canonization in 2016, there has been a renaissance of research and scholarship about her life, her mysticism, her works, and her place in spiritual theology and salvation history. *Named for Glory* is a significant American contribution to this revival and astutely examines the biblical, doctrinal, and missiological dimensions of her ecclesial mission while inspiring us to open ourselves in silence to the indwelling Trinity, who directs our own vocations, ecclesial missions, and unique paths to holiness."

— ***Bishop John O. Barres, S.T.D.,***
J.C.L., Diocese of Rockville Centre

"A deep, unique, and compelling account of the spiritual life of one of the most important saints for our times. Excellent reading for anyone seeking to grow in contemplative prayer and union with God."

— ***Fr. James Dominic Brent, O.P.,***
Author, *The Father's House: Discovering Our Home in the Trinity*

"In the Church today, *identity* and *mission* are key terms that show the deep longing of many for greater rootedness and meaning. This work presents Elizabeth, the vibrant witness that she was, as one who embraced life with zest and vigor, exactly in response to the deepening call of the Trinity over time. Indeed, it challenged me to go deeper into my own personal vocation. This book is an important Marian addition to the growing corpus of literature about this saint of our times."

— ***Fr. Francis Mary Roaldi,***
Franciscan Friar of the Renewal, Diocese of Paterson

NAMED FOR GLORY

Fr. Ignatius John Schweitzer, O.P.,
Julie Enzler, S.T.L., and Anthony Lilles, S.T.D.

NAMED FOR GLORY

St. Elizabeth of the Trinity's Identity and Mission

SOPHIA INSTITUTE PRESS
Manchester, New Hampshire

Cover by Updatefordesign Studio
Cover image: *St. Elizabeth of the Trinity* @ Archivio dell'Arte / Luciano e Marco Pedicini

Imprimi Potest
Very Rev. Allen B. Moran, O.P.
May 16, 2023

Nihil Obstat
Rev. Giles Dimock O.P.
May 3, 2023

Sophia Institute Press
Box 5284, Manchester, NH 03108
1-800-888-9344
www.SophiaInstitute.com

Sophia Institute Press is a registered trademark of Sophia Institute.

paperback ISBN 979-8-88911-290-7

ebook ISBN 979-8-88911-291-4

Library of Congress Control Number: 2025944595

First printing

Dedication

All the friends of St. Elizabeth of the Trinity

In Appreciation

Contents

PART II
NAMED FOR MISSION

PART III
OBLATION TO THE TRINITY— CAPTIVATED, CAUGHT UP, CONSUMED

PREFACE

Ye are Three, we are three, have mercy on us!
— Tolstoy's *Three Hermits*

THIS BOOK IS THE fruit of many conversations between three authors over the course of several years. As they pondered the wisdom of St. Elizabeth of the Trinity in prayer and conversation, a series of reflections emerged around the names that she believed were given to her. They organized these reflections into a kind of polyphony of thought. They could not have completed this effort without the encouragement of many friends. In a special way, they express their gratitude to Glenn Dickinson, who offered invaluable editing, and to Fr. Giles Dimock, O.P., who reviewed the overall theological effort to help clarify doctrinal ambiguities in the earlier drafts of this work. The end result is especially for those who seek deeper understanding of the spiritual doctrine of St. Elizabeth as a support for longer and deeper periods of prayer.

Though their theological backgrounds, love for prayer, and devotion to St. Elizabeth are similar, the diversity of their ecclesial roles and states of life have contributed to complementary threads of insight that may speak to different readers in different ways. Fr. Ignatius John Schweitzer, O.P., is a busy provincial promoter of the Dominican Laity, retreat master, seminary professor, and former Carthusian who spent years entering into great silence with St. Elizabeth. Mrs. Julie Enzler is a devoted wife, mother, and grandmother who discovered this Carmelite saint as a student at Franciscan University and has made her more widely known through courses and the careful translation of Sr. Giovanna della Croce's *Elizabeth of the Trinity: A Life of Praise to God* for Sophia Press. Professor Anthony Lilles, a loving and wise husband and father, provides retreat conferences, blogs, and podcasts on this twentieth-century mystic's spiritual mission around the world.

In this work, all three have bound together in common purpose to make known the wisdom of St. Elizabeth of the Trinity. All three believe that the renewal in mental prayer and holiness that the Church most needs today is found in her spiritual message. All three teach for the Avila Institute of Spiritual Formation and take up a mystagogical approach to theology, striving to lead the believer more deeply into the mysteries of the Faith. They have come to know for themselves how rich the writings of this saint are for this purpose. In this journey into the bosom of the triune God, they humbly entrust this work and those who read it to the intercession of the Virgin Mary and St. Elizabeth of the Trinity so that together we might abide in Eternal Light, Love, and Life.

NAMED FOR GLORY

Introduction

House of God, Praise of Glory, and Host of Praise

Who am I? Where am I going? What is it all about? How do I find true love? These perennial questions are all the more poignant in our confusion-filled times. The answer our hearts long for is not just a statement or formula rattled off, but one to be lived out as we "live the truth" (see 1 John 1:6). St. Elizabeth of the Trinity, the Carmelite Mystic of Dijon, has a spiritual mission to help us find this truth and she does so by captivating us with Christ. She wants us to know Him, for, no matter how painful the question, she is convinced that the answer abides in Him.

St. Elizabeth invites a living and personal conversation with Christ. The Lord Jesus addresses those who come to Him with a luring question of His own, "What do you seek?" (John 1:38). These foundational first words of Jesus in the Gospel of John receive a mysterious answer after the disciples, in turn, ask Him, "Where are you staying?" or more profoundly, "Where do you *abide* (*meno*)?" Jesus' response says it all in an open-ended answer addressed to us too, "Come and see" (1:39). The whole of the spiritual life is contained in this interchange.

St. Elizabeth, an astute reader of John's Gospel, knows where Jesus abides, "The only Son, who is *in the bosom of the Father*" (1:18). The Son has come to manifest to us this love in the bosom of the Father through His words and deeds (*Come and see!*) and to bring us to abide with Him in the heart of the Father in communion with the Holy Spirit. The interior life of the Blessed Trinity reveals itself and we are invited to enter — indeed, to plunge into — the divine depths of triune Love. This is where she wants to take us.

With her emphasis on silent contemplation and her devotion to "My Three and my All!" she is an expert fellow traveler along this simultaneously lush and rugged terrain of the life of prayer. This French nun conversed intimately about prayer with religious, priests, and laity alike, and we can find in her correspondence pathways toward the mysterious God who alone is *the* answer to these most existential questions of life. In her oblationary Prayer to the Blessed Trinity, we find Elizabeth's lived response to the triune God's beckoning that we seek all our answers in Him. Contemplation, as an experiential, loving knowledge of God, is "living the truth"; it brings us to Jesus, "the way, and the truth, and the life" (John 14:6).

Jesus, the revelation of the Father, comes to humanity through the faith of the Virgin, who conceives Him in her heart before she conceives Him in her womb. For the Christian, faith in Christ establishes one's identity and sacred purpose by giving a new name and a mission. Elizabeth's writings unveil three names that touch upon her own identity and mission in a way that connects her to the mission and identity of the Virgin Mary and, through Mary, to all believers: House of God, Praise of Glory, and Host of Praise. As each is a dwelling place of God for the praise of His glory, disciples are bound together in a communion to offer themselves over to Him as living oblations. This identity and mission is realized in the innermost being of the sons and daughters of God as we adore and savor the triune God Himself.

The names of St. Elizabeth of the Trinity disclose her identity and mission in the Church. There is of course her name *Elizabeth,* given first at Baptism and then again at her religious profession with the title *of the Trinity*. This name, given to her by the Church, serves as an icon through which her identity in the Lord unfolds. Her First Holy Communion occasions the fuller understanding of *Elizabeth* as House of God. Her awareness of being a dwelling place for God and a temple of the Holy Spirit deepens until she receives from St. Paul in prayer the name that she believed was to be hers for all eternity, Praise of Glory. In the final months of her life, a particular participation in Christ's saving work causes her to refer to herself as Host of Praise.

St. Elizabeth's identity and mission coincide in her names. Throughout her letters, House of God, Praise of Glory, and Host of Praise serve not only as terms of her sacred identity, but they also express doctrinal mysteries in a mysticism of *lived theology*. She refers to these mysteries to encourage and exhort her friends and family to holiness in God and to openness to His plan. In this way, the blossoming identity of St. Elizabeth of the Trinity reveals beautiful facets and a deepening of her spiritual mission for the whole Church.

Although she never abandons any of her names, each new name unveils a new facet and a new depth that prepare her for a special work. There is a conscious development in her self-understanding that shapes her spiritual mission. Her mission is to lead souls to total surrender and into deep silence where a transforming encounter with God awaits them. Her writings convey her self-understanding in a theological order that instructs, encourages, and exhorts, helping others enter this same surrender and silence.

St. Elizabeth's names are ecclesial and therefore sacred realities. In her oblationary prayer to the Trinity, "O My God, Trinity Whom I Adore," she identifies herself as someone to whom God has given Himself *Three* and *All*. That the saint should invoke the Trinity in this way evidences the spiritual development of her identity and what it means for growth in holiness. Elizabeth loses herself in God's own solitude and immensity with complete trust and abandonment because she knows who she is before Him. The polarity of losing oneself even as one comes into a deeper self-possession comes together in God's plan. His eternal plan expresses the eternal gift of self and eternal self-possession in the Divine Nature that is the very life of the Trinity. And this plan is being realized not only in the exterior events of her life but in the interiority of her own heart. This is precisely the meaning of the indwelling of the Trinity in the soul. The name *Elizabeth,* which she understood as "House of God," expresses this for her.

House of God grows into Praise of Glory through biblical contemplation. She never abandons her sense of being "House of God," but Praise of Glory helps her see more clearly her sacred purpose as a temple of the Holy Trinity. To this end, she believed God spoke to her through the writings of St. Paul. In a passage from Ephesians, the holy apostle revealed to her the name she came to understand that she would have in Heaven, Praise of Glory. From St. Paul's teaching, she recognized this was a call shared by all the faithful, and throughout her writings she invites her family, friends, and fellow nuns to make their own this new name which she had received. The gift of this name also confirmed more precisely her sacred identity before the immensity of God. She came to understand her purpose in terms of rendering God praise not only with words but with her whole being.

Just as her understanding of House of God develops biblically in her spiritual practices as a Carmelite nun, Praise of Glory flowers into Host of Praise. This new sacramental and liturgical development was born in her efforts to pray under the trial of acute and terminal suffering. A deeper conformity to Christ Crucified comes to the fore in her letters as she connects the agony of her final illness with the Mass. She becomes eucharistic. She offered herself as a host of praise and even promised to help those whom she felt were entrusted to her to make the same self-offering of themselves. This development was not an abandoning of her identity as Praise of Glory any more than Praise of Glory was a departure from being the House of God. Instead, each name inheres in the others so that each successive identity intensifies her union with Christ.

The Eucharist is the source and summit of this development. Her growing sense of identity in Christ reaches toward the mystery of participation in Christ's work of redemption. This is the summit of the Christian life — extending to others the saving work of Christ through the relationships and exigencies of our own personal existence. We do this by surrendering to the Lord our own struggles in faith, choosing to believe in Christ even in the face of what seems to be impossible. In the Eucharist, Christ takes these up and makes them acceptable to the Father as a participation in His work of atonement. This hope is firm even in the face of death. The sacraments and the liturgy bring us into this mystery — the mystery of the Cross, a Sacred Banquet, a pledge of future glory.

The Eucharist reveals St. Elizabeth's deepest identity in a manner that is spousal. Christ is the Bridegroom of the soul, and when we consider the unity of the Divine Persons, the whole august Mystery of the Holy Trinity may also be considered as Bridegroom. Through the discipline of contemplative prayer, Christ makes her spousal intimacy into a fruitful self-offering for the Church. From her infirmary bed St. Elizabeth gives expression to her own spousal longing through the words of St. Gertrude: "O Love! Love! Tarry not to accomplish my nuptials ... hasten to satisfy my longing ... Praise Thyself in Thee; praise Thyself in me and by me" (*Exercises of St. Gertrude,* read to Elizabeth on her deathbed).

St. Elizabeth entered these depths with the Virgin Mary who "kept all these things, pondering them in her heart" (Luke 2:19). Just as Mary's whole humanity surrendered at the words of the angel, St. Elizabeth's own humanity too becomes "a kind of incarnation" in which the Holy Spirit renewed Christ's whole mystery. It is through and with Mary that St. Elizabeth's spiritual identity in Christ grows into maturity. Mary is the gate that opens the deeper meanings of House of God, Praise of Glory, and Host of Praise, because each of these identities is related to Mary's own virginal maternal fruitfulness.

Our goal in these reflections is to journey deep into the significance of the names of St. Elizabeth of the Trinity to find signposts of hope for our own life of faith and to receive her invitation to share in her mission to live as a praise of glory. As is true of the dwelling places in St. Teresa of Ávila's *Interior Castle,* we see each name related to an ever-deeper substratum of her identity, and with each depth, a new expression of her mission and an unrepeatable instance of God's glory in the life of faith. Each name is another signpost that points to a secret that only God knows but that He yearns for us to share. Such are the horizons of the heart in whom dwells "the Furnace of Love."

This book invites the reader into St. Elizabeth's heart to find this Furnace. The progressive self-understanding that her names reveal unfolds like the structure of a church. Such a journey is always a pulling-back of the veil into the Holy of Holies and requires great reverence. House of God opens into the nave of her identity. Praise of Glory is the sanctuary, the deepest center and highest peak where the holy presence of God shines forth. Host of Praise is on the very altar of her heart, where an interior liturgy of offering and consummation unfolds. It is up to this altar and the oblation being made there that our pilgrimage ultimately takes us. There, great silences and mysterious canticles, divine impact and transformation, perfect praise and co-redemption all await. What is this place but "the bosom of the Trinity" and "the Furnace of Love"?

To arrive at this destination, this journey of meditations follows a tried-and-true map. Before entering into his cell, a Carthusian kneels before an image of Our Lady and asks her maternal permission and blessing. The steps he takes into the solitude of his dwelling place he takes under her protection. This journey has a sacramental and contemplative character in which Mary guides into the silence where Christ touches and transforms.

This book follows the same map. Before entering St. Elizabeth's heart, we open up the presence of Mary that permeates her whole message. Then, meditations on her letters serve as progressive steps ever deeper into her heart. Though the translations are our own, we provide abbreviated citations that follow the numbering for the letters and major works (HF for *Heaven in Faith,* LR for *Last Retreat,* P for *Poems,* L for *Letters*) as found in her *Complete Works* as edited by Conrad De Meester, O.C.D. and published by ICS. Finally, we open up the mystery of her identity and mission in relation to her great surrender in the oblationary prayer to the Trinity that, throughout this work, we will refer to as *Oblation to the Trinity* or *Oblation.* This surrender is into the bosom of the Father where St. Elizabeth wants to lead us because she passionately contemplates how Christ yearns for us to dwell there too.

To facilitate this pilgrimage, this work is divided into three parts. The first part of this work introduces the meaning of House of God, Praise of Glory, and Host of Praise through Elizabeth's reflections on the Virgin Mary. Within this Marian context, the second part of this work looks more specifically at her letters for the spiritual meaning of her names for herself and others. Finally, the third part of this work contemplates her *Oblation to the Trinity* from the perspective of St. Elizabeth's names and their Marian context to provide firm ground to those who desire to make this surrender their own.

In all simplicity, Our Lady and St. Elizabeth show the lived answer to our fundamental questions: Who am I? What do I seek? How do I love? Mary responds preeminently by her life of prayer, total offering of herself to her son, and spiritual maternity in the Church. From this great vantage point, the following meditations on the names of St. Elizabeth serve as an invitation to journey under the shadow of the Father into the same Furnace of Love where the answers to life's most important questions await us.

PART I

The Gate of Heaven

CHAPTER ONE

MARY AND THE THREE NAMES

THOSE WHO ARE DRAWN to understand and pray with St. Elizabeth begin well when they start with this Carmelite's devotion to Our Lady. At least this is true if one is to understand and pray with her names. House of God, Praise of Glory, and Host of Praise are most perfectly lived out by Mary. The Virgin Mother helps us ponder each name as the musical touch of God bringing her whole life into harmony with His divine plan.

The underlying reality of Elizabeth's self-understanding as House of God, Praise of Glory, and Host of Praise is present in nearly all her substantial thought even when she does not explicitly refer to these names. This is because her names undergird the mystery of who she is and her life with God. In a similar manner, Mary is likewise omnipresent in Elizabeth's writings, along with her names, even when they are not explicitly her focus. Truly, every Christian's identity in God is evidenced with greater clarity and depth in light of considerations of Mary's identity in God.

The distinctiveness of St. Elizabeth's Marian devotion serves as the point of departure for this exploration of her names. She lauds Mary as the Faithful Virgin, the Queen of Martyrs, and the Gate of Heaven, among other Marian titles. These titles are not entirely conventional today, though they receive a certain emphasis in this Carmelite's writings. Her emphasis underscores to some degree what is distinctive about her relationship to Mary, and this, in turn, offers a vantage point to explore St. Elizabeth's names.

Mary as Faithful Virgin sheds light on House of God or what it means for a soul to be a dwelling place for the Trinity (HF 39). The radiant witness and sword-pierced heart of the Queen of Martyrs as the Praise of Glory teaches souls in their daily duties and, in those more difficult moments where they find themselves at the foot of the Cross, to respond with their whole being to the will of God (LR 2, 40–41). Finally, the Gate of Heaven maternally ushers into Heaven each soul's self-offering as a host of praise in life and liturgy with the words "I rejoiced when I heard them say, 'Let us enter the house of the Lord' " (LR 41). On the fifteenth day of her last retreat, St. Elizabeth appropriates Christ's words to herself *Ecce Mater tua* (John 19:27).

> *She is there at the foot of the Cross, standing, in the strength and valor, when my Maestro says to me, "Behold your Mother." He gives her to me as Mother .... And now that He has returned to the Father, He substitutes me in His place on the Cross until I suffer in my body what is lacking in His passion, for His body which is the Church. The Virgin is there yet again to teach me to suffer as did He. She speaks to me to allow me to ponder His soul's last songs that no one else but she, His Mother, could know.* (LR 41)

St. Elizabeth learns to suffer in her own illness because she believed Christ conferred the Immaculate Virgin to her as Mother precisely for this purpose. Given to her as a gift, Mary stands by Elizabeth, and us, as Mother, helping to form us as House of God, Praise of Glory, and Host of Praise. In her holy maternity, Mary unites the suffering of Christ and the suffering of St. Elizabeth, and by extension, every Christian. In the shadow of her son's Cross, Mary learns as she is given to the Beloved Disciple as Mother. St. Elizabeth puts herself in the place of the disciple and invites her readers to do the same. Mary is given as Christ's gift to help us as we face death. Mary's motherhood extends over our faith as the Faithful Virgin, over our hope as Queen of Martyrs, and over our charity as Gate of Heaven, as she helps to complete the total offering of our lives and to usher us into that perfect loving union of Heaven. There, Love will have His final victory.

Faithful Virgin — House of God

Mary, the Faithful Virgin, embodies a mystery to be emulated if we too are going to be a fitting dwelling place for God. At the origins of the new creation in Christ and filled with a fullness of grace, Mary's virginal faithfulness and spiritual maternity open new horizons and possibilities of human life and prayer. Elizabeth learns from the Faithful Virgin to make these horizons of the new creation her own through the obedience of faith.

St. Elizabeth believes that Mary's faithful obedience draws the Trinity. The Trinity is the fountainhead from which springs forth all manner of new beginnings, new identities, and new *names*. Before such divine fecundity, a certain precondition is necessary: a radical freedom that is completely relinquished for God's will. This freedom is what Mary's virginal faithfulness attains. The faithfulness of the Virgin Mother allows divine freedom to be fully realized within the limits of her human freedom. God allows Himself to be drawn, to be moved by the faithful Virgin, who placed no limits on Him in any way, precisely because of His yearning to bring to completion His plan for humanity. Elizabeth describes:

> "Virgo fidelis," *the faithful Virgin kept all these things in her heart (Luke 2:19, 51). She stood so small, so recollected before*

> *God, within the secrecy of the temple, that she drew the favor of the Holy Trinity: Because "He has regarded his servant in her lowliness, all generations will call me blessed" (Luke 1:48). The Father was moved by this creature, so beautiful, so unaware of her own beauty, musing over how she should be the mother in time of Him of whom He is the Father in eternity.* (HF 39)

The greatness of divine freedom is drawn to the beauty of small and hidden Marian faithfulness. Mary's obedient faithfulness to God's word, that is her receptivity to God's delight in her, welcomes a new and deeper descent of the Word into her being. Earlier in this same work she says that believing in God's love is our great act of faith (HF 20). We see in Mary that this means humble attentiveness, a meek posture before God. It means not being distracted but staying silent, focused, or recollected on God's presence and plan. It means being hidden in the sacred, kept secret in the temple of God. As the "Spirit of love" comes upon her, the Faithful Virgin receives the Word in a manner that transforms her. Mary is thoroughly a woman of this new kingdom, the kingdom of God, this new dwelling place of God on earth.

Mary's virginity expresses a faithful readiness for the work of God. This readiness is not passive, it is actively open to God's coming to welcome Him and to respond to His desires. In the natural order, virginity is a kind of self-possession that is free to respond to love and life. In the order of grace, virginal faithfulness vigilantly conserves itself for all the new possibilities of God's saving work. It is open and ready for the ultimate end of the divine economy: perfect union and mutual indwelling between the creature and the Creator (*Catechism of the Catholic Church*, 260). This virginal attitude waits ardently to be filled by God, for fulfillment in God. This is not a posture of grasping for spiritual experiences but of serene submission to the total "otherness" of God and His will.

These characteristics of Mary's virginal faithfulness describe St. Elizabeth's ideal for the contemplative life, the dispositions for which the faithful ought to strive before God. This Marian obedience is possible because the Holy Spirit that descended on Mary descends on Elizabeth too.

St. Elizabeth unifies the visible and the invisible, public revelation and personal experience. What is revealed in the concrete historical particulars of salvation history is realized in the spiritual interiority of a soul's journey of faith. St. Elizabeth ponders the unity between the visible missions of the Spirit and the Word in the Incarnation and the invisible, spiritual missions of the Holy Spirit and the Word in the soul. What was accomplished definitively in history is extended in the mystery of the interior life. Adopting Mary's virginal disposition before the Trinity attracts the saving activity and presence of the Divine Persons.

The obedience of the faithful virgin to the Word of the Father sheds light on how contemplatives become, as did she, a dwelling place for God. The contemplative is a house of God in the sense of receiving God anew into her soul with her own virginal faith. Just as Mary welcomed God into her heart and womb through her pure and unbounded *fiat,* every contemplative welcomes the Lord through her own *fiat,* no matter how imperfect or incomplete. This mystery took possession of St. Elizabeth's identity when as a child she allowed her heart to be filled with wonder of what it means. She echoes the Marian mystery. We too echo Mary's perfect *fiat,* inasmuch as we interiorly acquiesce to God alluring us into deeper intimacy and lavishing us with a fullness of spirit, new potential, a mission, a new name.

With her own *fiat,* St. Elizabeth had asked for this virginal surrender in her *Oblation to the Trinity* when she prays, *Pacify my soul, make it Your heaven, your beloved abode, Your resting place.... my faith completely ready, wholly adoring, fully surrendered to Your creative action* (*Trinity whom I Adore*). The abyss of the soul deepens, becoming a vast dwelling place for her divine Beloved precisely through a faith that is obedient, a faith that translates into faithfulness.

Closely connected to this kind of faithfulness is Mary's recollected contemplation of the Word. The contemplative soul of Mary disposed her to the new thing God desired to accomplish in her. St. Elizabeth marvels over the Faithful Virgin's contemplative recollection. Elizabeth sees Mary's interiority captured succinctly by the Gospel's words about her, "Mary kept all these things, pondering them in her heart" (Luke 2:19):

> *"The Virgin kept these things in her heart": her entire story can be summed up in these few words! She lived in her heart and in such depth that the human gaze cannot follow her. When I read in the Gospel "that Mary hurried to the mountains of Judea" to fulfill her office of charity towards her cousin Elizabeth, I see her passing so beautiful, so calm, so majestic, so collected within with the Word of God.* (LR 40)

Absorbed in her contemplation of the Word, Mary moves in majestic beauty and peace. In her pondering heart, her spiritual powers are united. Moreover, this recollection unfolds at a depth beyond human understanding, at the depth where the Word dwells. The Word is the source of her peace. Absorbed in the Word, His majesty and peace radiate through the Virgin Mother in all her daily routines and in her loving solicitude for others. Mary magnifies God because of this indwelling presence.

The House of God as an Ideal Illumined by Mary

As it was with Mary, abiding with God as His dwelling is at the core of St. Elizabeth's identity. As a young girl, she was impacted profoundly by hearing that *Elizabeth* means "House of God." In the years that followed, the significance of this name came to disclose previously unseen dimensions. In November of 1903, on the feast of Our Lady's Presentation in the Temple, at the conclusion of the community's annual retreat, and after a period of intense spiritual trials, St. Elizabeth pondered the significance of her name as illuminated by Mary. She included her reflection in a letter to her sister. She wrote:

> *Just ponder what it must have been like in the soul of the Virgin when after the Incarnation she possessed within her the Incarnate Word, the Gift of God.... With what silence, what recollection, what adoration she had to bury herself in the depths of her soul in order to cradle this God for whom she was Mother. My little Guite, He is in us! Let us keep very close to Him, in that silence, with that love of the Virgin.* (L 183)

The meaning of Elizabeth's name as "House of God," as the dwelling of the Trinity, marked her. This "luminous ideal" was to be realized in daily life, as it was for the Virgin Mary, through a certain prayerful recollection of the Word. Just as Mary's adoration of the Word disposed her to transformation, so too St. Elizabeth. Clearly Mary was both a model and a standard for Elizabeth as she strove to bury herself *in the depths of her soul to lose herself in the Trinity who dwells therein.*

Elizabeth sees Mary as an example of what she herself strives to become: *I would like to respond ... by living on earth as did the holy Virgin, "pondering all these things in my heart," being buried, in a sense, in the bottom of my soul. This means to be lost in the Trinity who dwells there to transform me into itself* (L 185).

The pondering heart of Mary, absorbed in and expanded by the Word, and her response of faithful obedience, which welcomes a new indwelling presence of God, converge on what it means to be a house of God. Mary's faith and obedience welcome the descending Word into herself as Faithful Virgin and House of God and she is immersed more profoundly in the life of the Trinity. She is a house, not made of stones and mortar, but of a heart of love nourished by faith and obedience.

Faith and obedience are foundational for a house of God, and Elizabeth's other names proceed from them. God has made His dwelling with us, and this makes us a new creation, giving us a new identity in Christ, a new name. The kingdom of God is at hand, and indeed the kingdom of God is within (Luke 17:21).

Mary's virginal *fiat* discloses the relinquishing of the entirety of her being, soul and body, to God as His dwelling place, as House of God. She does this in full correspondence to God and His ways, making her a perfect praise of glory. And this, as extended to the offering of her whole life as a holocaust, makes her a host of praise. In her faithful and obedient simplicity before God's will, she radiates His presence, His glory, and His self-giving love. The simplicity of Mary's *fiat,* her yes to whatever the Lord desires, makes her whole existence a place of God, totally attuned to Him and His ways, and a selfless offering of unbounded praise. The Almighty has worked these marvels in His beloved dwelling place, Mary, the Faithful Virgin.

With Mary as her model of a contemplative, Elizabeth's name, House of God, became a guiding star, a luminous ideal, in her understanding of her own contemplative vocation. The connections she saw between the public events of salvation realized in Mary and the hidden graces of the contemplative life provided the basis for her encouragement of others in this same call. In the presence of Mary, pregnant with the indwelling God, we ourselves are formed to be a more fitting home for God with a similar Marian space in our souls for God's indwelling.

Mary is the living model of what it means for a house of God to remain in interior recollection, especially as she bears the incarnate God within herself and ponders all these things, keeping them in her heart. Mary's interior recollection, attentive listening, delicate love, receptivity, and docile response indicate her way.

Queen of Martyrs — Praise of Glory

As St. Elizabeth writes about living for the praise of God's glory, she often highlights the need to die to self so that God shines forth. Hence, Mary the Queen of Martyrs discloses the quintessence of a "praise of glory." Radiating God's glory requires the daily discipline of Christian life and death to self. Moreover, to praise is to make known or declare the glory of God. Martyrdom is literally "to bear witness," and as such it is an especially poignant example of being a "praise of glory," as one bears witness by making known the glory of God's love. St. Elizabeth connects praise with martyrdom, witness under duress. The Dominican preacher, Fr. Vallee, explained to her community that "Martyrdom is the response of any lofty soul to the Crucified" (L 214).

Elizabeth responds to Christ's love by immolation, a living disavowal of her own will, a form of martyrdom. It is the white martyrdom of an authentic Christian life. Through death to self, Christ and His love emanate most perfectly from us, making each as a "praise of glory."

Elizabeth looks to St. Paul. *I live no longer my own life, but the life of Christ in me. The life I now live in this body of death, I live it by faith in the Son of God who has loved me and given Himself up for me* (HF 28 and LR 16). Daily life's little martyrdoms are invitations to live in praise of God's glory. In every effort to place God before ourselves, His glory will shine forth. Even in little acts of *making haste* in service to others, as Mary did in the Visitation, or in receiving what the Lord has for us, like Mary at the Annunciation, we bear witness to the love of God. It is all of Mary's life that comprises her offering as the great praise of God's glory.

Martyrs present a perfect imitation of Christ and are models of Christian holiness for the whole Church. Under Mary's Queenship these witnesses affirm God's glory even in the face of injustice and violence. When the glory of God is revealed in catastrophe, their witness-unto-death offers the world a reason for hope. The Queen of Martyrs is a sign of hope. She is a sign of hope to the Christian who suffers for imitating Christ, and hope for the rest of the world in witnessing to the love that no evil can defeat. The Queen of Martyrs herself held her dead son in her arms. Yet, with undying hope she bears witness to the love that overcomes death. In a certain sense, every Christian act is meant to be a martyrdom — a bearing witness — a praising of the glory of God's victorious love over evil.

Mary's queenship allowed her to be perfectly present to her crucified son. She ministers in a similar way to every martyr, to everyone who bears witness to the crucified and risen One. She bears witness to the Love that conquers evil. The witness of the life of Christians, especially amidst suffering, speaks of hope. The Queen of Martyrs stands firm by the Cross as a sign of hope, a hope given to testify that our sufferings are not wasted but are united to the redemptive offering of Jesus and become praise. This hope, bright with the praise of God's glorious love, rests upon the victory that awaits such a self-offering in love *on the third day* for the Lord Jesus, and on the Last Day for Christians.

The Queen of Martyrs witnesses to the glory of the Son of Man who is glorified precisely on the Cross, where the will of the Father is accomplished. The task of a praise of glory is to share in this salvific work of love that puts God and others before self. The witness of Mary at the foot of the Cross ought to draw us and persuade us that, with her assistance, we too can love to the end.

The Marian Context of Praise of Glory in St. Elizabeth's Writings

St. Elizabeth is unequivocal: for her, Mary is *the great Praise of Glory* (LR 40). Even before Letter 191 to André Chevignard on January 25, 1904, in which she first mentions her "new name," *Laudem Gloriae*, Elizabeth begins to define life as *a praise of glory of the Trinity*. Later, during her final retreat, the notes of which form the text of her *Last Retreat*, Elizabeth placed herself before her Three, attuning her heart to the Maestro's indications. She was receptive to whatever He would whisper. It was through the Mother of the Word that God continued to reveal His designs to His little *Laudem Gloriae*. Sr. Elizabeth recognized Jesus as *the perfect Praise of Glory* (LR 2). And in Mary, who *has penetrated the mystery of Christ in its full depth* more than any other (LR 2), Elizabeth recognized *the great Praise of Glory* (LR 40). More than worthy of imitation or as an object of devotion, Elizabeth received Mary as her Mother. It was as a *daughter* that Elizabeth entrusted her formation as *Laudem Gloriae* to the Mother of Grace. This meant choosing to be, by faith, the Virgin's child, living out a true mother-daughter relationship with trust and confidence. *This Mother of grace will form my heart until her little one becomes the living, "stunning" image of her first born, the Eternal Son, the One who offered the perfect praise of glory to the Father* (LR 2).

The *Last Retreat*, recorded in her notebook for her sisters at the monastery, was carved out of her nights of intense physical suffering. In it, Elizabeth pondered all that preceded the sacrifice of the One crucified by love. He is the *perfect Praise of Glory* with whom no creature can compare. Yet His Mother participated in this mystery too, and through her St. Elizabeth discovered the path she should follow. In her prayer, Elizabeth accompanied Mary on the road into the hill country of Judea, the first stop in the journey toward Jesus' final surrender. Mary's Visitation to her cousin Elizabeth, along with her adoration at the foot of the Cross, helped define Elizabeth's sense of her own spiritual mission. Whether in ordinary service of others, like in the Visitation, or by a sacrificial offering of self, like at the Cross, death to self is the path forward for a praise of glory.

As Mary mothered *Laudem Gloriae,* the Carmelite learned to renounce her own will more and more completely. Mary's recollection and surrender illuminated Elizabeth's surrender to the particular martyrdom the Father offered her. Elizabeth was His specially chosen victim of love, and she looked to Mary as a model of how to embrace her own martyrdom. She identified with Mary as *predestined by the decree of Him who does all things according to the counsel of His will* to be *"the praise of His glory"* (LR 6).

The death to self that comprises the Praise of Glory's path forward is sustained by the prayer uttered in the abyss of one's heart. To all her correspondents, Elizabeth extolls the practice of *quotidie morior.* Such daily death to the *old man* is fundamental to the life of the Praise of Glory, allowing God to radiate in and through the soul as we *cling to Him by ... contemplation* (LR 8). The simplicity and unity of the gaze of the Praise of Glory renders her a splendor of God's glory, and her self-renunciation allows space for God to fill His creature with His own perfections and contemplate Himself there. This, Elizabeth writes, delights God's Heart (LR 8).

> *Then [the soul] dazzles with the "knowledge of God's glory," ... because she allows the divine Being to reflect Himself in her, "and all His virtues are manifest in her." This soul is the praise of glory of all God's gifts. She sings the* canticum magnum, *the* canticum novum *through all her acts, and her song thrills God in His very depths.* (LR 8)

The great canticle of Mary's life is St. Elizabeth's ideal for utter simplicity and self-forgetfulness rooted in humility and love. Our

Carmelite ponders the profound unity of Mary's being. Mary's interior silence was the foundation of the perfect conformity of her will with the will of God in every circumstance. Out of her silence and unity, her mundane acts were all transformed into a *canticum magnum* of praise. Wrapped in contemplation and bearing the hidden Christ Child in her depths, Mary sets out to serve her expectant cousin. Interiorly, Mary remains fully present to God dwelling within her as she calmly makes haste in splendor and beauty. Exteriorly, her outward acts of love and service express her interior, maternal adoration of the Word of the Father become flesh. The way she lives her divine maternity, the hidden harmony of visible and invisible movements of love, opens desirous souls to the vision and possibility of being with Mary a praise of glory of the Holy Trinity.

St. Elizabeth sees that, as it is for Mary, it can also be for each little Praise of Glory. Every mundane responsibility and occupation can be fashioned into a true song of praise, as the Praise of Glory turns from her noisy self and is buried in holy silence, present to God and surrendered to His will. Then All-Love abiding within will be made manifest to the world through loving service and in self-oblation. The denial of self, both for God in prayer at the foot of the Cross and for neighbor in mercy and service to him, increases our capacity for the Lord's self-revelation through us. *He must increase; I must decrease* (see John 3:30). Mary's song of praise, from her receptivity at the Annunciation to her humble surrender to God's will in her sacrifice at the foot of the Cross, allows God's glory to be magnified in and through her. So too, as we decrease and He increases, as we disappear through our practice of *quotidie morior*, will our lives become a song in praise of His glory.

Gate of Heaven — Host of Praise

A statue of *Janua Coeli,* Mary, Gate of Heaven, was one of Elizabeth's most prized religious articles even before she joined Carmel (L 188). In the months leading up to her death, St. Elizabeth turns to Mary increasingly under the title *Janua Coeli.* The final oblation of Elizabeth's life comes to its consummation as she becomes a host of praise and Mary is there to help the self-offering of love pass over into the next life. Mary is a gate to Heaven for Elizabeth. As her holocaust is being wholly consumed, the final consummation of love is being brought into the glory of the Beatific Vision. Whereas Mary as Faithful Virgin and Queen of Martyrs touched especially on faith and hope respectively, Mary as Gate of Heaven highlights charity. The consummated union of love has the last word as Elizabeth passes through the Gate of Heaven and God is all in all: *When I have said my* "consummatum est," *it will be she,* Janua Coeli, *who brings me into the divine courts* (LR 41).

In a letter written less than three months before her death, Elizabeth, with eyes fixed on Heaven, places at the head of her letter the phrase *Janua Coeli, ora pro nobis!* The rest of the letter accordingly unfolds under the gaze of Mary as Gate of Heaven. Elizabeth begins,

> Laudem gloriae *enters Heaven's novitiate this evening in preparation for receiving the habit of glory . . . This is what I will be taught: conformity, identity with my adored Maestro, the Man Crucified for love. Then I will be ready to fulfill my office of the praise of glory and sing already now the eternal* Sanctus *while I wait to go and intone it in the divine courts of the House of the Father. Let's train our eyes on our Maestro until our simple, loving gaze of faith separates us from everything and places a kind of veil between us and things of earth.* (L 307)

Mary is the novice mistress of Heaven, forming and preparing Elizabeth for the divine courts. This preparation involves beginning to sing the eternal *Sanctus*, already now, as a praise of glory conformed to Christ Crucified by love. Elizabeth's own life is coming to full consummation by loving to the end as her Maestro did. With the help of Mary, the Gate of Heaven, Elizabeth is better able to fix her eyes on things above. The Host of Praise is being consumed, and Mary helps Elizabeth especially in the handing over of herself that culminates in death's final surrender and her passing over into Heaven.

A month after this letter, Elizabeth crafted and gave to Mother Germaine a small handmade cardboard citadel that included an image of *Janua Coeli* standing at the door. On its flag are the words, *Citadel of suffering and of holy recollection*. Mary, Gate of Heaven, helped Elizabeth make that place of suffering also a place of holy recollection. Under Mary's care, Elizabeth's suffering was being transformed into a fortress of holy recollection.

Elizabeth pasted a poem of hers there as well.

> *I will be able to penetrate into this divine palace,*
> *Into this fortress, into this citadel*
> *Where the soul takes her rest in invincible peace.* (P 113)

Elizabeth eagerly longed to enter and be clothed in glory. The things of Heaven became her most substantive reality as she pondered Mary in Heaven, and as Mary helped her through the gate into eternal life with her son and for her son. *If the Blessed Virgin sees I am prepared, she will clothe me in her mantle of glory. Beatitude beckons me more and more. No other question than this exists between my Maestro and me. His whole concern is to prepare me for eternal life* (L 306).

For the Host of Praise, the holocaust of her whole life is consummated in death as she begins to pass over into heavenly realities. The

Host of Praise knows that suffering will not have the last word. As a host of praise, Elizabeth fixed her eyes on Heaven and saw that her suffering would soon be replaced with complete joy, peace, and happiness as she passed through the Gate of Heaven with Mary whispering to her, *Laetatus sum in his quae dicta sunt mihi, in domum Domini ibimus!* (LR 41), that is, *I rejoiced when they said to me, let us go into the house of the Lord!*

The Marian-Liturgical Context of Host of Praise in St. Elizabeth's Writings

The liturgical and eucharistic context of St. Elizabeth's use of *host* or *victim* became increasingly personal in relation to her own sufferings as she approached death. She understood that the task of the host of praise was to live as a self-offered holocaust, completely consumed by the Fire of Divine Love. Elizabeth had been captivated by St. Thérèse's *Act of Oblation to Merciful Love* in which Thérèse herself is victim and sacrificial holocaust. It was shortly after Thérèse made her offering that she suffered her first sign of tuberculosis, and a difficult spiritual night of feeling abandoned by God followed. St. Elizabeth built on this patrimony, with its ecclesial and eucharistic roots, as she pondered her own vocation as Praise of Glory.

As a host of praise, Elizabeth joined herself in her final agony, through the ministry of ordained priests, at their hands, to Christ's eucharistic sacrifice in order to be transformed into a living sacrifice of praise. Just as Christ the Victim offers Himself to be consumed by the Church in the eucharistic Host, Elizabeth offered herself in communion with His sufferings, to be utterly consumed by Christ as His prey. The House of God became Praise of Glory and then Host of Praise, Christ's victim of love. By offering herself, Elizabeth lived her participation in the royal priesthood (the priesthood of all the baptized, as distinguished from the ministerial priesthood of ordained priests). As Host of Praise, she joined her self-offering to Christ's eucharistic self-offering made in the priest's offering at the altar.

Elizabeth's first use of the name Host of Praise came about a year before her death, in a letter to Fr. Chevignard, when she asked him to remember her at the altar as he consecrated the sacred Host in the offering of the Mass:

> *When you consecrate the host where Jesus, "who alone is Holy," is made incarnate, please consecrate me with Him, "as a sacrifice of praise* (hostie de louange) *to His glory," so all my aspirations, all my desires, all my actions, render homage to His Holiness.* (L 244)

Here Elizabeth's own self-offering is taken up entirely in the offering of the divine Victim or Host in the Holy Sacrifice of the Mass. Just as Mary stood by the Cross at her son's Passion, so she stands in witness to Elizabeth, *substituted for Christ*, in her own passion:

> *He entrusts her to me as my Mother . . . Now He has returned to His Father and has substituted me for Himself on the Cross, so that "in my body, I might suffer what His Passion is lacking, for the sake of His body, the Church." The Virgin teaches me yet again to suffer as He suffered.* (LR 41)

Christ's entrustment of His Mother to Elizabeth enables her substitution for Him on the Cross. If Elizabeth is to *make up in her own body what is lacking in the sufferings of Christ* (see Col. 1:24) as a host of praise, she needs the assistance of His Mother who accompanied Him in His perfect offering. In her total self-offering, contemplation and the eucharistic liturgy coincide. She places her offering in the hands of the priest, in the bosom of the Church. Liturgical prayer and the sacramental life are ordered to this mystical participation in Christ's great self-offering by all the faithful under Mary's maternal solicitude.

In the maternity of the one *pierced by the sword,* the dying Elizabeth finds the courage and the strength to bear being a wholly consumed holocaust for Love. Mary inspires and strengthens Elizabeth's great desire to share everything with Christ and her great desire for the redemption of others: *[My] soul must be resolved to share fully in its Maestro's passion. It is one of the redeemed who in its turn must redeem other souls, and for that reason it will sing on its lyre:... "With Christ I am nailed to the Cross"* (LR 13).

This Host of Praise, substituted by Christ *for Himself on the Cross,* will learn from Mary how to suffer as He did.

> *"The queen stands at your right hand": this is this soul's attitude; she walks on the road to Calvary at the right hand of her King — crucified, annihilated, humiliated — yet always strong, calm, with great majesty, on His way to His passion "burning brightly with the glory of His grace."* (LR 13)

The Blessed Virgin will *help me hear the final song of His soul which only she ... could hear* (LR 41). The beautiful music of Christ's love opens the soul to the hymn of the divine silence. This is a redeeming silence in which humanity learns to glorify God even when facing death.

When St. Elizabeth described God as *a consuming fire,* it was at once a physical and spiritual description of this host of praise's encounter with God as her death approached. Her life was defined by terminal illness but, more essentially, it was consumed as a whole burnt holocaust offered to the Lord. Although her disease involved all the typical human difficulties of life in the infirmary and all the dynamics of any sick person's relationships with others, she offered herself to the Fire of the Holy Spirit as a spiritual holocaust.

Mary's spiritual maternity makes our human desires and sensibilities adequate for the designs of Divine Love ablaze in this consuming fire. Mary focuses on God's love even amidst great sorrows and heartache. At one point Elizabeth's own mother unsuccessfully prayed to our Heavenly Mother for a cure. Elizabeth understood her mother's discouragement and disappointment in the face of what seemed to be divine indifference. Yet she was so deeply convinced of Mary's maternal solicitude that she was innately convinced that something more extraordinary than a miraculous physical cure was unfolding in her dying.

Carefully diverting her mother's attention away from the disappointing results of her prayer, Elizabeth directed her to contemplate the love of God with Mary, encouraging her to join Mary at the elevation of the Mass so that, as the Virgin Mother offers her son to God, Marie Rolland might offer her daughter bound together with Mary in the same action of love: *Join the Virgin at the foot of the Cross offering your children together to the heavenly Father, "whose will is solely and entirely love"…!* (L 308).

This is a beautiful instance of Mary's humanizing influence on Elizabeth's spirituality. An earthly mother's sorrow and the suffering of her child have a place in the unfolding story of the soul with God, with the soul's offering of praise to God. Elizabeth, as she ends her days, adds to the titles she claims for herself this one: Host of Praise, as a victim and sacrifice of praise. The Paschal power of this name transforms even death. Without eyes of faith, the victim's death seems to be the end of the story. Suffering and death, however, do not get the last word in St. Elizabeth's self-offering. The Host of Praise points to the greater life in Heaven as she is offered to God and passes into His realm. With great rejoicing *Janua Coeli* gathers up Elizabeth's final earthly praises and becomes the open gate for her into the heavenly courts where she too will raise her voice in the eternal *Sanctus*.

CHAPTER TWO

To Be Virgin, Bride, and Mother

In the letters where she writes of the Virgin Mary, we find validation and development of St. Elizabeth's vision of Mary in the spiritual life. In these, Mary stands out especially as Virgin and Mother. In a way, Mary as Virgin and Mother cuts through the threefold identity we have just been pondering. A house of God is virginal in having a heart for God alone above all other loves and is also maternal in the outward pouring out of oneself in service of others from that source of love within. A praise of glory is virginal in seeking God's glory alone beyond all other glory and is also maternal in radiating and manifesting God for the good of others. A host of praise is virginal in the eschatological orientation to the things of Heaven and is also maternal in its spiritual fruitfulness for those on earth.

Mary is the supreme realization of all this. Elizabeth imbibes this reality and enters deeply into the mystery of the Christian life through her powerful awareness of Mary as Virgin and Mother. Thoroughly Marian in her outlook, her union is not greedily possessive; she is Virgin. Nor is her love selfishly barren; she is Mother.

As Mary conceived the Word in her heart even before in her womb, St. Elizabeth desires to conceive Christ in her heart, too. If Mary in her virginal maternity offers the Magnificat, St. Elizabeth wants to offer the praise of glory of the Holy Trinity. In both cases it is Christ who acts through His indwelling presence, and what He achieves perfectly in His Mother He also realizes in a different way in St. Elizabeth.

Mary is not only a model of what Christ can do; she also helps bring it about in those souls that are receptive to her. St. Elizabeth's devotion to Mary allows Mary's virginal motherhood to aid Elizabeth in becoming like her, a lyre under the Maestro's touch. Under Mary's spiritual motherhood, the Beloved dwelling in this Carmelite's soul draws her soul-strings into crescendo, an echo of what the Word of the Father communicates from the Cross. Only Mary can teach the soul to surrender to the Maestro's touch, because she stood in solidarity with Him when He unveiled the fullness of His saving mystery.

As Elizabeth dealt with the mystery of death, this song unfolded its beauty in her life, her letters, and her prayers for those she loved. Out of the depths of Elizabeth's misery, the Holy Spirit drew haunting movements of love, and the lyre's string of suffering was generously proffered to her Maestro in a manner that delightfully moved His Heart (HF 43). To illustrate this, we examine four letters, one from 1904 to a young seminarian (L 199), as well as three from 1906, to her friend Germaine de Gemeaux (L 278), to Mother Germaine (L 316), and to Mother Mary de Jesus, the prioress of the Carmel in Paray-le-Monial (L 306). These letters give rise to meditations on the mystery of Mary's motherhood in the vocation of virgin and mother, the connection between virginal love and renunciation, and, finally, the universal motherhood of Mary in the spiritual life.

The Vocation of Virgin and Mother

Virginity and motherhood offer rich insights into House of God as a name for St. Elizabeth. Just as the mystery of maternity fosters the intimacy and innocence that family life needs to thrive, the call to virginity and spiritual motherhood in the Church promotes the purity of her devotion and the fruitfulness of her mission. Elizabeth's call to be virgin *and* mother is connected to her understanding of House of God in this very way.

Looking to Mary, St. Elizabeth sees that the stronger the virginal love, the more maternally fruitful it is. How this is so is a theme of a letter she wrote to Abbé Chevignard. In an Easter greeting, likely written in April 1904, St. Elizabeth ponders the radical extent to which God uses virginal purity and maternal openness to life in His divine plan.

> *During this month of May, I will fully unite with you in the Virgin's soul. There, we will adore the Holy Trinity . . . I envision my Carmelite life as a twofold vocation: "virgin-mother." Virgin: espoused to Christ by faith; mother: saving souls, multiplying the adopted children of the Father, the co-heirs of Jesus Christ. Oh! how this enlarges the soul, like the infinite grabbing hold! . . . "God is free of all save His love." This word, which I believe is from Msgr. Gay, gives so much for my soul particularly in this time of the Resurrection where Christ conquers death and wants to remain our captive. . . . "I am sought, I am loved." Know that this is what is true. Anything else is not. Oh, how good to live by this life of the Trinity that Jesus Christ comes to bring to us! He declared that He is the Life and that He comes to give it abundantly.* (L 199)

For St. Elizabeth, adoration of the Trinity is realized through unity *in the Virgin's soul.* There is an implied ecclesial truth on which this unity and adoration unfold. This is to say, the inner life of Mary, characterized by both virginal and maternal love, is ordered to the adoration of the Trinity. To enter into the virginal and maternal movements of Mary's heart opens into adoration, a surrender and gift of one's life to God. It is from within this mystery of Mary, a virginal and maternal perspective, that St. Elizabeth envisions how God has called her to live as a Carmelite.

A twofold vocation: Virgin-Mother

St. Elizabeth connects Mary's virginal faith and maternal fruitfulness to the way God takes hold of and enlarges contemplative souls. Within the mystery of Mary, St. Elizabeth sees virginity and maternity as a response to God, her particular response as a woman and as a Carmelite. Adoration of the Trinity in the soul of Mary dedicates her soul to God's desire for mutual possession and divine generativity.

The Life of the Trinity unfolds in a soul given over to this Marian adoration of God. Just as Mary's human motherhood and virginity are taken hold of and expanded through the purity and generous response of her faith, so too the Carmelite and, by extension, all who consecrate themselves to God in various ways. For God to grab hold of a soul means that He implicates it in His saving mission, and to do this, He must expand it beyond its limited natural capacities. Within the soul of she who *magnifies the Lord*, we might speak of a new magnificence of soul, a supernatural greatness that magnifies God's fruitfulness in the world. If faith allows God to grab hold and expand a soul in this way, St. Elizabeth sees adoration of the Trinity by faith as the way that Our Lady and Carmelites give themselves to God in love.

She has developed this idea of love from the beginning of this letter. God's freedom to give Himself in love is the whole context for her thoughts on unity, adoration, virginity, and maternity in the soul of Mary. Intending to solicit empathy for God, she cites the proverb from Msgr. Charles-Louis Gay, a nineteenth-century Oratorian, bishop, and popular spiritual writer, often quoted among the nuns in her community, *God is free from all save His love* (L 199).

The proverb she cites imposes a limit, at least in a certain sense, on divine freedom. She attributes to Christ the desire to be captive to our love. Such captivity underlines the necessary negation contained in Msgr. Gay's proverb. Divine freedom is not arbitrary or heartless in its purpose. A fullness of eternal freedom operates in the order of charity in which humanity has a special place. It is an eternal fullness of freedom directed by Divine Love for humanity. This fullness operates in Mary, in her virginity and her maternity. In her and through her son, God desires to possess and to be possessed by the human soul. St. Elizabeth's attributing to Christ the desire to be held captive reveals the divine freedom for mutual and reciprocal possession. At the same time, the metaphor of captivity evokes faith's response to God's freedom.

Faith that seeks relationship is living, animated by love. It does not only believe that God exists and what He says but also believes for His sake. In this sense, it is directional: it leads to Him. Faith that frees the soul of everything except love allows us to participate in Christ's Resurrection because the Resurrection expresses God's freedom to love. To understand in what sense God is free from all save His love, we find in the Bible that God *cannot deny Himself*. Creatures suffer the imperfection of being able to contradict their image and likeness to God. This allows us to conclude, with St. Elizabeth, that God's desire for captivity, so to speak, is not a deficiency but a perfection of love that evokes love. St. Elizabeth seems to follow this line of reasoning when she continues: *Christ, Conqueror of Death, desires to be our captive. He desires this so that we might resurrect with Him, passing through this earth "free from all save our love"* (L 199).

The Resurrection allows God to give Himself in a way that communicates his own freedom "from all save His love." In making Himself captive to humanity, God places no limit on freedom for humanity but gives humanity the freedom to be like God, to love free from all save Love.

The virginal soul espoused to Christ by faith is freed from everything but love. St. Paul makes this point in his First Letter to the Corinthians, "I want you to be free from anxieties. The unmarried man is anxious about the affairs of the Lord, how to please the Lord"

(1 Cor. 7:32). There is a virginal freedom from the concerns of this world; the soul is concerned only with pleasing the Lord. It is being freed from all except love.

This *freedom from all* but the Lord's love is something to which all Christians are called. It also constitutes a life lived virginally for the Lord. Those who consecrate themselves through a vow of evangelical chastity (or else are consecrated as virgins by the Church) are special witnesses to this freedom for the whole Church. St. Elizabeth is one of these living signs. Yet faith in the Risen Lord always avails a participation in Christ's virginity in which all the baptized share in different ways. Insofar as a soul participates in Christ's virginal manhood, He purifies its love and faithfulness.

In all its forms, such virginal freedom is an exclusivity of focus on the Lord stemming from the bond of love. The anxieties and distractions of life that risk consuming our minds and hearts are dropped into their rightful place under the Lordship of Jesus Christ. The One Thing Necessary, time and time again, needs to be intentionally enthroned in our lives. Only then are the rightful concerns of life in the world put in their proper perspective, allowing us to take up our daily tasks fruitfully as acts of love for the Lord.

Love by faith and you will be freed of all else. When love is the main driving force of all you do, all other concerns drop away. Then the virginal love of the Lord leaves its mark on all you do in your family, community, and daily work. In the life of prayer there is an exclusive virginal focus, concerned only with love.

Such virginal freedom is possible because of God's freedom to love the soul. Virginal dedication is formed in the pattern of God Himself who is free of all save His love. How this divine love is communicated to the soul is foundational to St. Elizabeth's thought. We must truly know that the deepest reality in life is God's love for the soul. Everything else is secondary. She explains: *"I am sought, I am loved." Know that this is what is true. Anything else is not. Oh, how good to live by this life of the Trinity that Jesus Christ comes to bring to us! He declared that He is the Life and that He comes to give it abundantly* (L 199).

To know that God's particular love for oneself is true and to reject everything contrary to it opens up the life of the Trinity for the soul. This kind of knowledge, knowledge that one is loved by God, comes from faith. In other words, it is not a feeling or an intuition, but a movement of will in response to God's invitation. Anyone who would live by this love wants to be *held captive, grabbed,* and *enlarged* by God because He has found home in this soul. This love is the life of the Trinity that Christ offers to *be free from all, save our love.*

Spiritual maturity is realized in the use of one's full freedom to love others sacrificially. Such love finds expression in the many different kinds of relationships that we share with one another. Of these, the highest and most demanding, but also the most meaningful, are fatherhood and motherhood, if even on the natural level, even more on the spiritual level of grace. This freedom for love that the Risen Christ offers in faith serves as the intrinsic link between freedom and virginity, on the one hand, and love and fruitful motherhood on the other.

Virginal motherhood love constitutes St. Elizabeth's heart as a home, with sacrificial love as its sacred center. We have seen that Mary's soul is presented as a home, a household, a place where this Carmelite intercessor can go to adore the Trinity. Because she finds her home there, St. Elizabeth is also a house of God for those Christ sends to her. Her adoration of the Trinity is ordered not only to the glory of God but also for the good of those entrusted to her. This spiritual motherhood furthers the salvation and sanctification of souls, even while remaining virginally hidden in her life of prayer and sacrifice.

St. Elizabeth speaks of her spiritual motherhood in terms of her share in the work of the salvation of souls. Because St. Elizabeth sees the Immaculate Virgin conferred to her as Mother — *Ecce Mater tua* (LR 41) — she understands that she is entrusted with a mission of spiritual maternity over the souls the Father confides to her for all eternity. Elizabeth works to bring souls to Him who will be formed according to the vocation of praise of glory. This is a theme that we find in the same letter to André Chevignard to which we have been referring, *I also envision my Carmelite life under this double vocation: "virgin-mother." Virgin: espoused in faith to Christ. Mother: saving souls, multiplying the adopted children of the Father, the co-heir of Jesus Christ. Oh, how this almost boundless embrace enlarges the soul!* (L 199).

St. Elizabeth sees her whole way of life as soul-enlarging. Formed as spiritual mother in the soul of the virgin, she wonders over the increase of God's adopted children, formed into the image of Christ. If the virginal quality of the soul is marked by the exclusivity of love, then the maternal quality of the soul is marked by love's breadth and expansiveness. Maternal love especially enlarges the soul because it reaches out to all the children of God in an *almost boundless embrace* (L 199).

This has a profound application. Each soul is a whole world unto itself, and this is multiplied countless times, in every soul, held as it is in existence by God. It is worth pondering that the weight of one's own unique subjective existence — the particular richness of one's own interior life, the singular taste of one's own perception of reality, the crucial importance of one's own aspirations, the peculiar depth of one's own desires, the familiar intimacy of one's own personal relationship with God — is multiplied many billions of times over.

The weight of my own "I" is measured on the scales of existence with the totality of each and every individual human person throughout the ages. Together, each stands as a totality in relation to God. I approach God in this context, with countless others as numerous as the stars of Heaven. As God receives my prayer and attends to my soul, His gaze simultaneously pierces into the innermost core of every individual soul He holds in existence. We can echo Elizabeth's cry, *Oh, how this almost boundless embrace enlarges the soul!* (L 199).

The maternal dimension of Elizabeth's vocation brings with this breadth of charity the personal tenderness of love. For us too, it is especially the souls commended to us in our daily interactions that can expand and enrich our souls. As we enter into the lives of others with all their particularities and charm, our souls are enlarged and enriched. The virginal exclusivity of the Lord is not in tension with this, but even enhances it. It is God who is All-Love at the center of our virginal love, who empowers the maternal tenderness and expansiveness of love found in our relationships with others.

The House of God who seeks God with a virginal love is not caught up in a selfish pursuit, closed off from others. Love is at the center of the House of God, and He expands our hearts to make space for others within our house. It is from virginally seeking solely Him that we draw forth the love that is maternally concerned for others. Here, we confront a great paradox that takes us above the natural order: the spiritual virgin is the spiritual mother.

Mary as Virgin-Mother is the supernatural ground, model, and channel for all spiritual maternity and virginity. St. Elizabeth as virgin-mother plants herself in this Marian soil, and she intentionally receives her sense of identity and mission from it: *I also envision my Carmelite life under this double vocation: "virgin-mother."*

Hence, with and through Mary, she is also a model and channel of grace for others, precisely as House of God. Since the first outpouring of the Holy Spirit at the Annunciation, the Christian vocation has virginal and maternal roots regardless of one's state in life. To this end, the Virgin Mother Mary forms St. Elizabeth of the Trinity to renew the mystery of virginal motherhood into a dynamic place of encounter with God. Elizabeth also tells her brother-in-law *during this month of May I will closely unite with you in the soul of the Virgin. Together there, we will adore the Holy Trinity* (L 199).

In the fruitful breadth of her charity—in the house of her soul—Elizabeth unites closely *to us in the soul of the Virgin.* In the enclosure of Mary's virginal heart, together with one another as the many children of our Blessed Mother, we adore the Holy Trinity. A powerful image that captures all this is that of religious women and men and Christian faithful finding refuge under Mary's mantle. This image is a beautiful depiction of Mary as House of God. She is both virginal and expansively maternal. She is a home for God and also for us.

Virginal Love and Renunciation

Having considered how the virginity and motherhood of Mary impacted St. Elizabeth of the Trinity as House of God, we now consider how virginal love and renunciation, when practiced within the mystery of Mary, impacted her identity as Praise of Glory. Our meditation proceeds from a letter that St. Elizabeth wrote to Germaine de Gemeaux, a young friend. This is not directly a Marian letter, but the themes of virginal love and renunciation develop ideas that we set out in chapter 1 when we discussed the Queen of Martyrs and the Praise of Glory.

The letter refers to a difficult personal context that allows us to connect what she advises Germaine in relation to the praise of glory and what she will elsewhere reflect upon about Mary as Queen of Martyrs, for example in her *Last Retreat.* Just before the section of the letter that we will comment on, St. Elizabeth tells her young friend that since March, she has been committed to the infirmary. She has Addison's disease, a fatal illness only recently discovered and without any known treatment at the time.

The disease advances rapidly. St. Elizabeth explains to Germaine that she suffered a severe attack on Palm Sunday that no one believed she would survive. However, after receiving the Sacrament of the Sick, at the time called Extreme Unction, to everyone's surprise, her condition improved. Relief from some of her symptoms now allows her to spend her time in the infirmary in constant and deep prayer, and it also allows her to write a response to Germain who wrote her a get-well letter filled with questions about vocational discernment. Nevertheless, St. Elizabeth is suffering from fatigue in the face of certain death. This accounts for the urgency and seriousness of the letter. At the same time, St. Elizabeth baptizes this whole reflection to her young friend in profound mystery. At the top of the letter, a single line reminds us of our previous discussion on the House of God: *The Father is charity, the Son is grace, and the Holy Spirit is self-communication.*

The letter brings together the life of the Trinity and death to self in St. Elizabeth's virginal devotion to Christ. This quote comes from the liturgical celebration of Trinity Sunday. It is a reminder of the Divine Indwelling that highlights the distinctions of the Divine Persons in the unity of their being. Yet, the further reflection on this point is only made much later in the letter, after bringing together renunciation and virginal love. This coming together opens up space for the praise of glory, a space she goes on to illustrate with trinitarian imagery drawn from the Annunciation. This reference connects powerfully with the thoughts that she will later develop concerning the Queen of Martyrs while also offering an application of them to address her young friend's specific circumstance. Bearing in mind that Elizabeth has been in the solitude of the infirmary for more than three months *with nothing but love*, we find her speaking out of her own virginal love to Germaine. In June 1906, St. Elizabeth offers words of counsel that apply for vocational discernment as well as the whole Christian way of life:

> *Dear little Germaine, you were given very good advice. Be faithful to your resolutions. Take up the way of sacrifice and renunciation. Throughout the whole Christian life, this should be the great law. This is even more the case when it comes to a soul like yours. For, whatever His plans for you may be, you aspire to follow the Maestro very closely. Always live with Him within. This requires enormous mortification. To unite oneself to Him ceaselessly like this, you have to know how to give everything to Him. When a soul is faithful to the slightest wish of His Heart Jesus, in turn, is faithful in caring for it, and a sweet intimacy is established between them.... I am asking Him always to be the Maestro who instructs you in the secret of your soul. Little Germaine, pay full attention to His voice and call to mind that, when He takes His place in a heart, it is to live there "alone and set apart." You get what I am saying. I am not speaking of religious life, which is a great separation from the world. Instead, I speak of detachment, of purity putting a veil over everything that is not God, permitting us to adhere to Him ceaselessly by faith ... May the Father cover you with His shadow, and may this shadow be like a cloud that envelops you and sets you apart. May the Word imprint His beauty in you, in order to contemplate His Self in your soul as in another Self. May the Holy Spirit who is Love fashion your heart into a little furnace that delights the Three Divine Persons through the ardor of Its flames ... [God] loves you so much, little sister. He so wants you for Himself whatever the path you must follow. How our soul needs to draw strength in prayer, especially in mental prayer, this intimate heart-to-heart, in which the soul passes into God and God passes into the soul to transform it into Himself.* (L 278)

From the selected passages of this letter, we see that St. Elizabeth does not rob Germaine of the powerful moment for spiritual maturity that vocational discernment requires. *Whatever His plans for you might be ... whatever path you must follow* signifies the great discretion that the young nun has regarding how God may call her friend. She also does not fail to firmly propose the Gospel: faithfulness in mortification, renunciation, and sacrifice is the *great law* in the Christian way of life. On this point, Elizabeth proposes spiritual death, a life of continual renunciation, as necessary for union with God: *Always live with Him within. This requires enormous mortification. To unite oneself to Him ceaselessly like this, you have to know how to give everything to Him.*

St. Elizabeth grasps that mortification, a process she refers to as death to self or forgetting self, unites a soul to God. Renunciation is an act of faith that helps us die to self, forget self. She sees that a new intimacy with Christ is at stake in this effort. The condition for this intimacy is attentiveness to His slightest wish, His least desire. Such attentiveness is what mortification, knowing how to give everything to Jesus, makes possible.

To have this kind of attentiveness to Him, we must disavow and not sanction desires, habits, and attachments that draw us away or impede us from what He desires. She knows that when sinful or frivolous attachments dictate our lives, our dignity and integrity are threatened and often even lost. She wants to protect Germaine from this as Germaine discerns her vocation. When Christ finds us and offers Himself as a new way of life, our priorities completely shift, and St. Elizabeth wants Germaine to live by these — for when even the slightest desire of the Lord is our priority, our lives, no matter what we discern, are filled with great meaning. This is what St. Elizabeth wants for Germaine. This is why, rather than simply offering counsel regarding how to discern, St. Elizabeth emphasizes this spiritual death that comes through faithfulness to renunciation and sacrifice.

Christ's own renunciation of all that does not give glory to the Father is the basis of all truly Christian renunciation. He only did the will of the Father. This loving dedication allowed Him to glorify the

Father even from the Cross. Associated with this praise of glory is His Mother whose *yes* to the will of the Father also implied a *no* to all competing whims that might distract her from the love of God. In this letter, St. Elizabeth does not explicitly make this Marian connection between renunciation and praise. It is, however, there implicitly. Mary is a hidden presence in renunciation as an act of faith that pertains particularly to the Praise of Glory, who must decrease so that He may increase.

To understand the connection between death to self and praise, we must return to St. Elizabeth's teaching on the Queen of Martyrs that was developed earlier. In that consideration of *Last Retreat*, 40, among other texts, Elizabeth's powerful connection between Mary's titles as the Queen of Martyrs and the Mirror of Justice was evident. Elizabeth's sense of contemplative prayer involves being *buried* in the Trinity.

She suggests that the recollection evoked by God's presence occasions a kind of spiritual death. St. Elizabeth speaks of an adoring recollection as a burial. The implication is that something about oneself dies in the deep silence of adoring recollection before God. Something about oneself needs to die and be buried in this prayer. This is because St. Elizabeth understands spiritual death is a pathway to intimacy, a new motherhood. She sees in Mary's silence, recollection, and adoration a going down into a tomb where God has buried Himself too. This tomb is for her just as it was for Mary, at the bottom of her soul. Buried in this deepest depth, Mary comes to cradle this God for whom she was Mother (L 183).

This suggests the pondering recollection of Mary is pregnant with a paradox. In the depths of Mary's heart, her silent adoration brings together spiritual death and life-giving motherhood, like the grain of wheat that falls into the earth and dies so that it may bear much fruit. As Mary is entombed in prayer, within her is born a life of a new motherhood. This is a spiritual embrace of the Word in a death to everything that came before and in a birth to new maternal affection. Mary's whole existence is endowed with new meaning, expanded with a new kind of love. The growing mystery unfolds within her. The Word grew in her womb, but the Word also enlarged her heart for others as it does for us too.

Elizabeth's language about contemplation speaks of self-abnegation, for she means *buried* in the sense of laying herself in a tomb. It is the same language found in her *Oblation to the Trinity*. It could be said that St. Elizabeth contemplates the Trinity, in all Its life, love and light, as the tomb in which she dies to self. She brings together the superabundant life of the Trinity and the death to self that contemplation demands with her metaphor. Beyond a metaphorical connection, she sees a Marian connection in the Queen of Martyrs: the lowly handmaid of the Lord who puts God and His will before herself even to the point of going to the Cross of her son is a model for the interior soul.

Mary as Queen of Martyrs is a concrete visible model that reveals the pattern, the form of mental prayer and union with God. Mary's heart-pierced contemplation of her son's will informs her preveniently redeemed and maternal love so that it actually directs the witness of every martyr in the age of the Church; hence her title Queen of Martyrs. This means that Mary in her hidden martyrdom (the sword that pierces her heart), her spiritual death at the Cross in union with her son's bodily and spiritual death, shows the righteousness of God, revealing the truth about sin and the truth about God's love. This spiritual death is the culmination of a lifetime of renunciation, first in evidence in the Annunciation itself.

The Virgin's *yes* to God implies a life of renunciation that is itself a martyrdom, that is, a witness with her whole life, reflecting a light not her own. Whereas in her *Last Retreat* Elizabeth refers to the title

Mirror of Justice, she had already proposed a similar insight with her sister nearly two years before this letter to Germaine: the Blessed Virgin is *a martyr in her heart* who shines with *kindly light, the Morning Star* (L 197a) who shines in the heart of her friends.

Associated with her son and in her own creaturely perfection, the Virgin Mary is the Praise of Glory. Her virginal love shines with the light of her son precisely because she is a martyr in her heart through all the virginal renunciations that lead to the Annunciation and to the Cross. In the context of renunciation this means complete selflessness. Although she did not need to be purified of sin as her redemption was effected at the moment of her conception, she was nevertheless transformed as she renounced herself to follow her son. This means that renunciation gives God space not only to purify but also to transform a soul until it shines forth as His praise of glory.

In her letter to Germaine, Elizabeth points to this transformative power of renunciation, implying the truth of her insights at work in Mary's hidden, spiritual martyrdom. Martyrdom is a witness unto death, and the life of the Queen of Martyrs helps us see that a praise of glory offers this to Christ throughout a lifetime of renunciation, even if without the shedding of blood. What exactly is the connection between renunciation and virginal love of Christ to which the Queen of Martyrs witnesses?

St. Elizabeth describes and illustrates this with Mary at the foot of the Cross, leaving an invitation to ponder this question. Freely embraced self-denial made out of love for the Lord is the precondition, the spiritual space in which God cooperates with the soul to fulfill its deepest desires. These are stirrings of heart that the Holy Spirit causes. In this space, the soul gives God the permission He seeks to remove obstacles to His love, bringing into a new wholeness the body, soul, and psychological powers, and intensifying the light of His radiance in the spiritual life. This is why St. Elizabeth rightly sees the lowly handmaid of the Lord radiating God even as she gives her *fiat* in renunciation of all else but God's perfect will: *I am the handmaid of the Lord, let it be done unto me according to your will* (see Luke 1:38).

We can sometimes unconsciously think of ourselves as too sophisticated for renunciation, especially renunciation of the world. We rightly emphasize that the world is good and has a fundamental role in our relationship with God. At the same time, we can sometimes be blind to the ways it may be holding us back from love of the Lord. True virginal love, however, strikes a sharp and decisive *No!* to all that may hinder or distract from a deeper union with the Beloved. Seeking God's glory alone means renouncing one's own glory; this is the life of a praise of glory. It requires great self-abnegation. In letting God shine upon others through us, we must choose Him above self.

How could the infinite God not be enough for us? Of course He is! Many saints express this same sentiment. The pithy words of St. Teresa of Ávila on the matter are used by Elizabeth more than once as the heading of her letters: *God alone suffices* (L 218, L 249, and L 324). This constant clinging to the Lord by faith is spousal in character. It involves healthy detachment from all that is not God so that one's heart is free for the Lord — He who alone suffices. In her letter to Germaine, Elizabeth encourages her young friend to have her heart set apart for God alone: *When He takes His place in a heart, it is to live there "alone and set apart" ... I speak of detachment, of purity putting a veil over everything that is not God, permitting us to adhere to Him ceaselessly by faith.*

In His place in the soul God lives *alone and set apart*. God's own divine solitude and holiness animate the virginal soul. Each act of faith, each sacrificial deed, wounds the soul with the beauty of God culminating in an exclusive intimacy that exceeds even spousal love. It is not about what we set aside but about making space in our hearts for the beauty of the Lord. The Lord God is *a jealous God,* a jealous Lover. St. Elizabeth helps us see what this means for us and our practice of renunciation as ordered to what she calls *such sweet intimacy*.

To get at this intimacy, we must uncover the latent Marian reflection in this letter, Marian in the sense that it is incarnational filled with references to the Annunciation that open out to Christ's work of atonement. Throughout her writings, St. Elizabeth develops a connection between the visible and the invisible, the historical and the mystical coinciding in Mary. What is only latent in this letter she develops with more explicit force in the meditations she offers in *Heaven in Faith* and *Last Retreat*. To Germaine, right in the middle of her letter, Elizabeth draws from the biblical imagery that echoes the Annunciation to offer her a blessing:

> *May the Father cover you with His shadow, and may this shadow be like a cloud that envelops you and sets you apart. May the Word imprint His beauty in you, in order to contemplate His Self in your soul as in another Self. May the Holy Spirit who is Love fashion your heart into a little furnace that delights the Three Divine Persons through the ardor of its flames.* (L 278)

To be overshadowed by the Father, to be imprinted with the beauty of the Son, and to be on fire with the Holy Spirit echoes the grace of the Incarnation when the power of the Most High overshadowed Mary and she conceived by the Holy Spirit. Taking this blessing offered to Germaine together with what Elizabeth originally wrote in the *Oblation to the Trinity,* the connection is even more convincing. In that prayer, St. Elizabeth also speaks of being overshadowed, but more explicitly offers her soul to be *a kind of incarnation* of the Word, one in which Christ *renews* in her humanity His whole mystery. In other words, Christ not only takes flesh, but acts through her flesh to extend His work of atonement and glory. The language clearly connects to the Annunciation so that Elizabeth affirms a connection between the visible mission of the Son in history with His spiritual mission in the soul in mystery.

Though there is little direct reference to Mary in her letter to Germaine, the blessing that Elizabeth offers her is profoundly Marian. Similarly, though this letter does not explicitly mention the praise of glory, it nonetheless unfolds the basic principles at work in this name. Just as Mary's virginal *yes* to the words of the angel leads her by love to stand at the foot of the Cross, St. Elizabeth wants Germaine to pronounce her own *yes* in the pattern of Mary, a pattern that is open to participation in and witness of Christ's whole work of redemption: *those who He has known and predestined to be conformed to His Christ, crucified by love* (LR 41).

The connection between virginity and martyrdom in Mary is effected by the overshadowing of the Father, the imprinting of the Son, and the enflaming of the Holy Spirit. Among the Carmelite spiritual masters, the most profound moments of awaking and mystical union are described with language drawn from the Annunciation. In the French school of spirituality, connections are made between what is revealed in the public moments of revelation in the Bible and what God does in the secret of the heart. For St. Elizabeth, the Marian moment of union culminates in an association by grace with Christ's work of redemption. This association is what a praise of glory expresses.

This association is realized and sustained in contemplative prayer. To express this, St. Elizabeth speaks of the soul "passing into" God. For St. Elizabeth, the vocation to be praise of glory is a passing into the life of God that associates us in Christ's work of redemption. Through contemplative prayer, her whole life is implicated in or passes into Christ's work of redemption through the indwelling of the Trinity. She writes: *How our soul needs to draw strength in prayer, especially in mental prayer, this intimate heart-to-heart, in which the soul passes into God and God passes into the soul to transform it into Himself* (L 278).

Contemplative prayer, prayer where one lets go of self and all earthly cares and enters into stillness before the Lord, is a source of strength. The Carmelite Rule declares that it is in such silence that the soul finds strength. This is why St. Elizabeth goes beyond counseling Germaine to ask for strength. Such petitionary prayer is foundational because it helps incline the soul to the right attitude of heart it needs for deep silence before the Lord. Yet, to receive the strength of the Lord, one needs to seek a deeper kind of prayer, one that goes beyond the vocal expression of a petition and rests in an adoring posture before the mystery of God. More specifically, it is through surrender to divine love that God strengthens a soul. This is what St. Elizabeth means by *passes*.

Here, *passes* goes beyond divine action that the soul passively receives. By previously speaking of renunciation and mortification, St. Elizabeth also draws attention to the soul's own grace-informed actions in God. This establishes a mutual and reciprocal relationship, a spousal intimacy with God that a virginal soul not only receives but also participates in. For St. Elizabeth, the soul passes into God even as God passes into the soul. Human agency is united to divine freedom by grace.

Intimacy of the mutual passing of the soul into God and God into the soul demands strength that only God can give. A principle found in Carmelite spiritual teaching is that when two wills draw together, the greater the mutual possession and likeness they share, the more they suffer in love to give themselves one to the other. Each lover must be strong in his resolution and desire for the other, or the desire for intimacy remains unrealized and frustrated. In this line of thinking, the union of love is the result of a suffering that endures the separation and requires strength to sustain its resolution. If this is true in human relationships, what kind of strength is required for a soul to be resolute before God? Faithfulness to God demands a strength only God can provide, divine strength. Intimacy with God involves a new movement of grace in the human heart which communicates this strength until the soul is strong enough to surrender itself, to pass into His great mystery. Contemplative prayer is about welcoming this strength and making this surrender, allowing oneself to pass into God.

St. Elizabeth describes this suffering intimacy as a mutual flowing: the soul flows into God and God flows into the soul. This flowing intimacy involves transformation, a greater likeness to God by grace, in which God's strength empowers the soul to suffer especially in the silence of contemplation. As contemplative union matures, the soul fully becomes the image and likeness of the Beloved to whom she has given herself and who she has welcomed into her own depths. This passing of God and the soul into one another, this intimate heart-to-heart in which the soul is transformed by a life and love beyond itself, such is the goal of St. Elizabeth's spirituality.

With her single-hearted focus on God, belonging more to Him than to herself, His presence flowing in her and hers in Him, she shines as a true praise of glory. There is a paradox to this exclusive, spousal love for the God who is a jealous Lover. It is this: the more we love God alone, the more our love for others grows and deepens. Striving to live for God alone, St. Elizabeth shines with His love as she ends her letter with affectionate kisses for others: *Kiss your dear mother for me ... and also Yvonne, to whom I send a very affectionate kiss.* And to Germaine, she says, *I am your sister for all eternity*. Yet all this remains within the scope of her secret intimacy with God: *A Dieu, my dear little Germaine, "may our life be hidden with Christ in God."* Indeed, she notes that this union with others occurs only in God, in whom *our souls meet and become "but one" through the Heart of Jesus, in the Holy Trinity*. In the end, it is precisely when we are united that our single-minded and virginal purpose of willing God and His glory alone reaches its culmination. We form an even greater praise of glory when we are together, united, not alone.

Mary's Universal Motherhood in the Spiritual Life

The Mother of Mercy speaks through St. Elizabeth of the Trinity. Undergoing severe agony in the final weeks of her life, the young Carmelite allows Mary to speak through her to her prioress, as well as to every soul who stands in the face of calamity. Behind this letter is Jesus' own generosity to us. He does not withhold His own Mother from helping us and strengthening our faith when everything seems to be falling apart around us. He supports us even as He consumes us as His host of praise. Just as Mary helped Jesus make His very first offering to the Father as He entered the world, so the Virgin has come to help us make an offering of our lives too. Elizabeth addresses these lines to her prioress on Mary's behalf.

> *"Ecce Mater Tua" . . . .*
> *Upon entering the world, Jesus made His first oblation to the Father from the embrace of my arms, and now He sends me to receive yours! I bring you a scapular as a pledge of my protection and of my love, and also as a "sign" of the mystery that will be worked in you. My daughter, I come to complete your "being clothed in Jesus Christ" until you "walk in Him," who is the royal and luminous Way, with the Father and the Spirit of love, into the very depths of the Abyss. I come until you are built up in Him who is your Rock, your Fortress. I come until you are*

> *"affirmed in your faith." I come until your faith is affirmed in the immense Love who plunges the very ground of your soul into the great Furnace. My daughter, this all-powerful Love will accomplish great things in you. Believe in my word, the word of a Mother. This Mother thrills in seeing with what particular tenderness you are loved. Oh, remain in the deepest core of your being and behold Him who comes fully armed with gifts. The abyss of His love surrounds her like a cloak: behold the Bridegroom!*
>
> *Silence!*
> *Silence!*
> *Silence!* (L 316)

Just as Mary was involved in Jesus' oblation, so too she is involved in Mother Germaine's oblation as a host of praise. The final threefold *Silence!* suggests we must consider the contents of this note as more than a mere exercise in pious imagination. This message discloses something of the Virgin Mary's concrete particularity. In Hebrew, superlatives are expressed by repetition. *Silence!* three-times commanded witnesses to the voice of the Jewish handmaid who conceived in the great silence of her own faith. Great love can be received only in great silence; the greater the love, the greater the silence into which we must enter in order to receive it. The Mother thrills in seeing with what *particular tenderness you are loved.*

Through the pen of St. Elizabeth, Mary the Mother of God comes to strengthen Mother Germaine in the oblation of her life; to affirm Mother Germaine's faith; to call to mind the blessings that she has already received; to consider the hope-filled future of her life; and to invite her into the greatest of silences before the Bridegroom. Through the lips of Mary, the present, past, and future converge in silent adoration before the Lord.

Written on the anniversary of Mother Germaine's vows and investiture in the scapular of Our Lady, Elizabeth presents this day not in terms of Mother Germaine's personal accomplishment but in terms of God's tender love. This love evokes deep silence. This gift appears as humble cloth, a scapular. Yet to the eyes of faith, it is a protective garb and a clothing with Christ Jesus. Faith sees the gift of God that remains otherwise hidden from unaided human eyes.

Through very subtle inferences, the Virgin of Nazareth connects this anniversary with the Annunciation. Just as Gabriel declared that "the power of the Most High" would "overshadow" the maiden betrothed to Joseph son of David (Luke 1:35), so now St. Elizabeth explains that *immense Love* will *plunge the very ground* of Mother Germaine's soul. Just as Mary's whole being came under the power of God, the very core of Germaine's existence is also plunged into *the great Furnace.* Just as the Word became flesh in the humble purity of a poor virgin, so in the hidden poverty of religious life, the prioress' whole being burns with eternal meaning.

Mary comes into our lives to help us descend into the great silence in which she herself welcomed the Holy Spirit. She comes to us standing under the Cross, and she waits for us to hear Jesus say, "Behold, your mother!" (John 19:27). If we welcome the Mother into the home of our hearts, she will help us remember, affirm our faith in the particular tenderness and immensity of Jesus' love, and enter more deeply into that silent attitude that is ready to respond to Him. With the docility of this silence, even amidst adversity and total calamity, *He who is mighty will do great things.*

Indeed, we too must suffer the immensity of God's love plunging us into His fiery furnace as a host of praise. There is a purifying aspect that is both necessary and very painful. As long as self-promotion and self-occupation reign within, we lack total freedom in giving, in offering our lives for the glory of God and the good of our neighbor. Yet, God not only purifies us, but He raises us to participate in His very life of love, to burn with the same love with which He burns from all eternity. His love for us is brought to consummation precisely as His fire of love consumes each one as His victim of praise.

Just as Mary bore Jesus into the world, she bears Jesus anew into each one of our hearts as a house of God. As we are transformed, God brings to birth in us new desires that burn in our hearts so intensely they move us into a new way of being and acting. This is the life of Christ in us: a life ablaze in the power of the Holy Spirit, a burning desire for a deeper intimacy with Christ. An interior desire is ignited, to do something for Him in return for all that He has done for us. We allow Him to radiate forth as we each are a praise of glory.

Finally, a passion flames up so that our neighbors and friends might glimpse something of the joy and freedom that we have come to know from the new life given from Heaven. These desires or flames in the furnace of God's love will consume our whole existence if we welcome them with the silent love that allows them to grow. This is a Marian silence, a faithful response that she comes to affirm. When these flames of love set fire to the very ground of our existence, we finally begin to realize the greatness of what we are called to be in this life and the next. This mystery of a life ablaze with love is the mystery of Christian holiness, holiness as a living sacrifice, love wholly consumed, spiritual worship, a host of praise.

SUMMARY

MARY AS A GATEWAY OF GOD'S PLAN FOR ALL HUMANITY

ST. ELIZABETH LIVED WITH her mind and heart in Heaven. This is captured particularly in her retreat *Heaven in Faith*. Her heart was fixed on Heaven from an early age. Yet was she therefore prone to live disengaged from the mundane in her everyday life? Precisely the contrary. She enjoyed warm, touching relationships with her family and religious community. She was empathetic and charming, and she knew how to connect. Those around her felt noticed by her and felt that they were the object of her sincere affection. In these ways, she engaged the ordinary affairs of daily life with tremendous love.

At the same time, St. Elizabeth's joyful engagement of life was not intimidated by the mystery of suffering and death. In her devotion to the Crucified One, she was filled with reverence before God's presence in earthly difficulties and sufferings. It is said that she never concerned herself with secondary causes. She interceded with tender concern for the whole world. Her devotion to the Queen of Martyrs, touched as it was with tender care, gathered all these facets of her spirituality, as she entrusted herself to the Gate of Heaven's maternal care and guidance.

Her Marian devotion can only be rightly interpreted against the charm, empathy, social intelligence, courage, and prayerfulness of her character. Her devotion was fully human and fully alive. The maternal love of the Gate of Heaven accounts for this. Just as in the account of man's creation in Genesis *woman* revealed to *man* the truth about his humanity, the Mother of God is a humanizing factor in Catholic spirituality. The Handmaid of the Lord surely experienced the heights of contemplation, yet this contemplation could hardly be *dis*-incarnate or abstract. Precisely in gazing upon and caring for the Word-made-flesh in the simplicity of their home in Nazareth, the Gate of Heaven contemplated the mystery of God-with-us, Emmanuel.

In Catholic spirituality, we recognize all that is good, holy, and true about humanity in her virginal readiness to generously respond to God. We see this again in her maternal care and solicitude. We also ponder what is most holy in humanity in her patient courage amidst the many dangers and trials that she confronted in faith. Humanity shines at its best in her gentle strength, her tenderness and compassionate love toward those who suffer. The great purpose of humanity is revealed through her incarnating spiritual realities in ordinary life, especially in the home. Similarly, the spiritual life in the Catholic tradition does not disregard domestic life or the virtues of womanhood. Instead, it seeks to sanctify these as did the Virgin Mary: by ordering them to devotion to her son. Doing everything out of love for Jesus makes even the most ordinary human acts echo into eternity as part of the great eternal *Sanctus*.

St. Elizabeth helps us see how Mary's virginal motherhood carries, as it were, the contemplative soul. Mary forms the contemplative in the tension between mysterious polarities. The one who would devote himself to sincere prayer must become both single-hearted and broad-hearted. Such a soul must learn to love God alone and likewise love everyone He sends. Such a soul must be both self-possessed and self-giving. In the face of these powerful tensions, Mary carries the soul with the same maternal love with which she loved her son.

When we accept the gift of her motherhood from Christ, Mary the Faithful Virgin informs our natural capacity to ponder, to welcome, and to embrace and receive life. Mary, Queen of Martyrs, exercises her queenship over the soul, and she helps it prepare to offer itself as a praise of glory even when that causes suffering. She is also mysteriously present as a gate, a passageway, when each host of praise fully participates in Christ's Passion, and love is consummated. The eucharistic and contemplative soul enters through Mary as *Janua Coeli* into the eternal *Sanctus* of the House of the Lord. St. Elizabeth's names reveal how this devotion applies to the life of every believer.

House of God

Elizabeth takes Mary as an exemplar of interior recollection, as a house of God. She bore God in the home of her womb for nine months and in the depths of her soul as well.

> *The attitude of the Virgin during the months she spent between the Annunciation and the Nativity is a model for interior souls, those beings in whom God has chosen to live deeply, in the bottom of the bottomless abyss. In peace, in recollection, Mary went out and lent herself in everything! How she divinized even the most mundane things! This is because in and through everything the Virgin continued to adore the gift of God!* (HF 40)

To realize their great calling, contemplatives need to acquire the Virgin's attitude. This attitude is one of welcoming receptivity to God by faith. The Divine Indwelling is the source of this attitude: His presence in the depths of the soul evokes this openness. God dwelling in Mary allowed her to radiate Him in all she did because, in everything, she clung to Him. It is in this vein that St. Elizabeth understands all that Mary did had God as its source and returned to God as its end. *The adorer of the gift of God* shares in this Marian existence, becoming himself a house of God.

The Marian attitude allows itself to be drawn by God until the Trinity becomes the soul's specific gravity. This fosters readiness to move deeper into His mystery in every circumstance. With such faith, each circumstance becomes a new opportunity to be open to God in a new way. All *interior souls,* who live from *the depths of the bottomless abyss,* tend toward these depths of God. This in turn allows the soul to welcome new magnitudes, new depths of divine presence.

This interiority is particularly marked by a certain femininity. The natural inclinations of womanhood are raised up by God in Mary to a supernatural mystery. We see these spiritual inclinations enfleshed in a pregnant woman. A pregnant mother enjoys a silent, hidden communion with the person she bears within herself. As intimate and meaningful as this is, God raises these natural inclinations even higher. When pregnant with the Word of the Father, Mary embraces a Divine Person within her body and soul. The Mystery-made-tangible that fills her womb is the fruit of God's working in her innermost being. She becomes a dwelling place, a home for God, not only in the order of what is natural to pregnancy, but even more, on a new spiritual plane of intimacy with God.

To be the House of God in this Marian light means to dwell with God in the interior cell of the soul, even in the midst of activity. The Virgin Mary, pregnant with the Word-made-flesh, embodies interior recollection through all her activities. Recollection is, for her, an intimate dwelling with the Trinity who dwells within. Dwelling within with Word-made-flesh, making her home with the Trinity, imitates Mary's attitude as the Mother of the Redeemer. Such recollection, more than a conscious state or psychological achievement, is at once an intimate and tender attitude as well as one that requires resolve and courage.

The Carmelite ideal of interior recollection is realized in this very attitude. As a Carmelite, her monastic cell was St. Elizabeth's spiritual home. But this home was a visible sign of an interior reality. What attitude captures such a spiritual existence? For St. Elizabeth, it is the attitude of the Virgin Mary. The more she makes this Marian attitude her own, that is, this virginal readiness for obedience to God's plan and intimacy with Him, the more the Trinity makes Its home in her. The soul, as is true of her cell in the convent, becomes a place of intimacy with God, a spiritual home where she dwells, as Mary did with Christ through the Spirit in the shadow of the Father.

One more aspect that we must mention before going further is the fruitfulness of the Divine Indwelling that constitutes a soul as a house of God. St. Elizabeth expresses this in a poem that she wrote, probably also for one of the nuns in her community named Sr. Mary of the Trinity. The poem is entitled *Feast of the Trinity* (P 79). Elizabeth was appointed Sr. Mary's *angel* and had the mission of providing a word of encouragement on Sr. Agnes's patronal feast day. In this poem, St. Elizabeth draws an analogy between the fruitful prayerfulness of the Virgin Mary and that of Sr. Mary. In both instances, the image she portrays of the humility of the Trinity before prayerful humanity is astonishing — occasioning both great wonder and desire for boundless graces:

In deep silence, in ineffable peace
This divine prayer never will cease.
Her soul enveloped in most brilliant light,
Mary, faithful Virgin, stands day and night.
A crystal her heart, reflecting the divine
The Host within, Beauty absent decline.
Drawing down heaven, behold! the Father,
Entrusts her His Word, making her Mother.

Now she by the Spirit of Love is in-shadowed,
To her come the Three and all Heaven is opened,
Knelt down, prostrated, adoring the wonder,
Of God Incarnate in this Virgin Mother.
On Mount Carmel another Mary says Fiat,
A great communicant, her soul all enveloped
In profound, mysterious contemplation,
Surrendering to God, her sole occupation!
Upon her shines a brilliant ray of light
Of the Father's Face a reflection bright.
As at Nazareth, 'neath God's divinity
Before this virgin, down kneels the Trinity.
"O Full of Grace, the Angel would be I,
Always singing praise to heaven on high.
Aren't you wrapped, Mother, in Infinity?
Keep watch in your soul over little me,
With such recognition my heart is consoled.
To God in silence my prayer has been told.
Asking for you His great invasion,
The descent of the Three, consummation!"

The fruitfulness of the House of God is established by a Divine Invasion. St. Elizabeth describes the transformation of the soul and its fruitfulness in the Divine Indwelling in terms of the Mystery of the Incarnation in Mary. Specifically, she connects the reception of Holy Communion with the Mystery of the Incarnation. It is a curious invasion. Just as God allows Himself to be tenderly enveloped by Mary and Mary is enveloped in His mystery, so the soul is invaded with the reception of Holy Communion if it is vigilant in its faith. The invasion is not a violent overthrow of human freedom, but the vulnerable, intimate coming of Christ into the heart, making the soul fruitful with the Holy Spirit. Engendered not principally by what the soul does but by the astonishing thing that God does, this invasion of the Trinity into the soul consummates profound union with God. All fruitfulness comes from this invasion. From this Marian perspective, this fruitfulness of God in the soul can be said to be the basis of a spiritual motherhood in the Church.

Praise of Glory

St. Elizabeth explicitly recognizes Mary as the most perfect realization, after Jesus, of being a praise of glory. True glory is a manifestation of one's inner being, radiating out in splendor. Mary, as a praise of God's glory, does just that with respect to God: she is a pure radiation of God dwelling deep within her soul. Mary is beautiful, *so serene, enveloped in such majesty as breathes at once both strength and sweetness* (LR 41) — and all of this because she dwells so deeply in the interior of her soul. *Her soul is so simple.* Within it are movements so deep that they can but leave us astounded (LR 40). Mary, a praise of glory, is so transparent to the God who dwells in her soul that God's glory is free to emanate out from her without blemish and without reserve. This is the contemplative's ideal. Liturgical texts, saints, and many theologians recognize that Our Lady bears something of a resemblance to Lady Wisdom: "She is a reflection of eternal light, a spotless mirror of the working of God, and an image of his goodness"; "She is a breath of the power of God, and a pure emanation of the glory of the Almighty" (Wisd. 7:26, 25).

And indeed, Mary is so free from any movements of independent self-assertion that she allows the Lord to fully work through her. This is the radical freedom that the prayer of faith makes possible. She is so transparent to the Lord and His power shining forth that she can truly proclaim, "He who is mighty has done great things for me" (Luke 1:49).

Those who would grow in contemplative prayer also find in Mary a model for humility, self-forgetfulness, and freedom. Such freedom of heart gives the Lord freedom to act, to do great things. As Elizabeth observes, *She is so authentic in her humility because she is always forgetful, unaware, free from herself. "The Almighty has done great things in me; henceforth, all nations will call me blessed"* (LR 40).

How was Mary able to live like this? The answer is important for the soul who wishes to follow Mary in being a praise of God's glory. Two things are emphasized by Elizabeth in characterizing Mary as a praise of glory. First, Mary dwelt in simplicity in the depths of her soul, and this means that Mary is a praise of glory because she is so perfectly a house of God in familiar intimacy with the Lord. Second, Mary lived out the simplicity of her *fiat* as she gave a wholehearted and simple *yes* to whatever God's will brought her. It is that simplicity that allows God's Being to radiate out from her, unencumbered as she is by self-centered motives and actions.

Dwelling in the Depths

By dwelling in simplicity in the depths of her heart, where her being was most intensely in contact with God's being, Mary was able to bring forth from these depths a likeness of God's own being and attributes. She was able to draw out, from the deep well of her soul, the pure and refreshing living water Jesus promised in giving the Holy Spirit.

In the depths of her soul, Our Lady was perfectly attentive to God's subtle promptings and inspirations, completely attuned to God and His ways. If glory is the radiation of being, the Virgin exists as a praise of God's glory, because she was wholly open and transparent to the presence and power of God radiating from her. She lived in a love much deeper than any passing demands of the moment could disturb. She allowed the deepest mysteries to lay claim on her so that even life's most difficult circumstances could not distract her from her Beloved. The subtle pulsations of His

Spirit, the slightest inclinations of His will emanating from His depths extend through her and out to the world. For these reasons and many others, St. Elizabeth describes the Virgin Mary as *the great praise of glory of the Holy Trinity* (LR 40).

A Wholehearted *Yes*

As the great praise of glory, the Faithful Virgin is lovingly obedient. Filled with the Holy Spirit, she makes haste to visit her cousin. The call of interior recollection does not neglect or abandon external things. Instead, it maintains an interior attentiveness in the midst of external demands, giving the whole heart in love to God and His will. The call is to abide always with God, in His temple which is in our soul, while being obedient to the requests of God's love in the world. This is how a contemplative, a praise of glory, brings His presence into every activity and situation, whether visiting a neighbor in need or facing a difficult situation.

The Faithful Virgin maintained this devotion to God's presence even in the face of her son's Cross and spiritually participated in its mystery. Simeon's prophecy regarding the piercing of Our Lady's heart makes us aware that recollection of God's presence in the face of suffering shares in Christ's work of atonement. Mary, the Virgin Mother, active contemplative, teaches us in the most intimate and personal way to share in Christ's own praise offered to the Father for the salvation of the world, as another praise of glory in our own day. The Queen of Virgins is the Queen of Martyrs, her heart pierced by the sword, interior soul that she was (LR 41).

Host of Praise

House of God having been taken up into Praise of Glory reaches full liturgical, eucharistic expression and consummation in Host of Praise. Like the Virgin Mary, Elizabeth has surrendered herself to God as His prey, to be wholly handed over to Him and His purposes. In the end, her final surrender of love takes on the connotation of being consumed by love. In being consumed as Host of Praise, Elizabeth is completely handed over to God as her love also reaches its final consummation and she reaches into Heaven. She leans toward the eternal Wedding Feast of the Lamb and hears marriage songs sung from the Cross. The songs of love she hears then ... are they of earth or Heaven? They are so mysterious. As Mary stood at the foot of the Cross offering her son to God the Father, now she bears up Elizabeth in her passion. Mary knows well suffering's mysterious love songs:

> *She is there, at the foot of the Cross, standing, in strength and valor when my Maestro says to me,* "Ecce Mater tua." *("Behold your Mother.") He entrusts me to her as my Mother .... And having now returned to the Father, He substitutes me to take His place on the Cross that I might suffer in my body what is lacking in His passion, for His body the Church. The Virgin is there yet again to instruct me how to suffer like He did. She reveals to me, she helps me hear the final canticles of His soul that she alone, His Mother, heard.* (LR 41)

Mary *learned from the Word Himself how those chosen by the Father as victims, hosts, should suffer, those whom He has resolved to associate with His great work of redemption* (LR 41). She herself is a victim, a host of praise. Elizabeth sees herself as *victim* and *co-redeemer* but only in union with Jesus, as Mary herself was (L 300). From her first months in the convent, Elizabeth was drawn to Mary in her role as victim with her son, that is, in the mystery of participating in Christ's redemptive suffering. She celebrates Our Lady of the Seven Sorrows and in the courtyard of the monastery there is a statue of *Mater Dolorosa, for whom I have great devotion* (L 94). Mary is a host of praise united with

Jesus; *Jesus, Mary, how deeply they loved one another: the entire heart of one made itself flow into the heart of the other* (L 188).

Our Lady's union of heart with Jesus on the Cross is both virginal and maternal. This union, now made fruitful and poured out for others, becomes liturgical, echoing the songs of the heavenly Wedding Feast. Through the Gate of Heaven, through Mary, Elizabeth enters deeply into this virginal and maternal sacrifice of praise. Mary draws each soul into the same mystery of union, through all the rich contours of human relationships and sufferings of everyday life.

St. Elizabeth describes Mary accompanying her on her *Last Retreat* as her novice mistress vigilantly keeping watch for *Laudem Gloriae*'s readiness, *Hostia Laudis*'s surrender. Her death is oriented to an entrance, a clothing, a profession. It is no earthly habit but the mantle of glory with which Mary will clothe this host of praise. It is no earthly cloister into which she leads her but to a face-to-face with Christ, to Elizabeth's final consummation.

> *I set out [on my voyage] with the Blessed Virgin on the Eve of her Assumption in preparation for eternal life.... This retreat is going to be, as it were, my novitiate for heaven ... If the Blessed Virgin sees me ready, she will clothe me in a garment of glory. Beatitude draws me more and more. There is only talk of this between my Maestro and me. His whole occupation is to prepare me for eternal life ... My soul will sing His canticle of praises while waiting on the Bridegroom to say to her, "Come, my praise of glory, you have sung sufficiently here below, now intone your canticle in My eternal courts, under the shining brightness of My Face."* (L 306)

With her face unveiled, bathed in the light streaming forth from the face of Christ, Elizabeth is reaching the final destination of her life's journey. Her human existence is brought to fulfillment as House of

God, Praise of Glory, and Host of Praise. Elizabeth lived out her vocation under the guidance, formation, and motherhood of the Virgin Mary. This is our call, too. We can count on St. Elizabeth also to help us with her prayers, discovering that her words apply to us as well: *We will rendezvous under her virginal mantle* (L 214). Whether under Our Lady's mantle of glory or under the mantle of the lowly handmaiden of the Lord, there we will join in the eternal *Sanctus* and hear the mysterious songs of the Wedding Feast of the Lamb.

PART II

Named for Mission

INTRODUCTION

WE HAVE SEEN HOW St. Elizabeth understood the names House of God, Praise of Glory, and Host of Praise in relation to the Virgin Mary. Let us now consider how Elizabeth applied these names to herself and to others, especially in her letters. Each chapter in part II contains reflections on certain letters that elucidate one of these names. Because the names are related to each other and integrated throughout her letters, certain themes are repeated. Each repetition enriches the others with its own theological and spiritual insights. What unfolds is symphonic.

We are mysteries even to ourselves. We discover the truth of who we are through an authentic gift of self. A name, touching on who we are, indicates the gift we give to others in giving ourselves. Such a name hints at the mystery we are. This is especially true when God gives the name. St. Elizabeth received her names from God in different ways and at different points of her journey. Each name denotes her response to God's self-gift and flows from her identity in Christ Jesus. As we mature in the spiritual life, we live according to who we have become by means of God's grace. Elizabeth's names divulge more particulars of her identity in God and elucidate how she lived well her own life's contours. Her name provides stability to her identity in the midst of life's changing circumstances: for instance, any of life's various sufferings can be experienced as random occurrences or they can be recognized as invitations to live more fully the call to be a host of praise.

Our spiritual name roots us in our God-given identity by orienting our daily life toward the fulfillment of our God-given mission. Our own identity, considered in light of what Elizabeth saw in her three names, sets us on the path of fulfilling our baptismal identity and of God-empowered living, life in the Spirit. Such a meditation permits a particular kinship with Elizabeth's own calling and places us under her patronage, her formative influence.

CHAPTER ONE

HOUSE OF GOD

HOUSE OF GOD UNFOLDS her baptismal name, Elizabeth. In spiritual theology, notions like the depths of the soul, ground of the soul, abyss of the soul, or center of the soul, each capture something important about the profundity and interiority of the human soul and its love. House of God embraces all these — a house has its inner chambers, basement, and foundation — yet it also emphasizes the personal. *Someone* lives in a house.

The *Someone* who dwells in our soul is the living God, and He has designs and purposes; He sets our house in order. The Beloved who comes to us is also Lord. And He will be Lord over every portion of His house. As we have seen, the response of our *fiat* is key here. We are His house where He is to reign both as Lord and as Beloved. Much of the Christian ascetical life consists in God setting His house in order: rearranging the furniture, stripping away old wallpaper, restoring and renewing as is needed, and kindling a blazing fire in the center fireplace. The house of the soul needs to be set in order and warmed up — and its fire ignited. The Divine Guest has His own ways, and our cooperation and *fiat* allow Him to have His way with us, so that He will make His home in us.

At Baptism the Fire of Divine Love is lit in the center of the House of God, and it will grow and blaze forth with full ardor as a praise of glory. As this fire consumes the holocaust, the host of praise, suffering is transformed in love's flame. Jesus' and our suffering, suffused with love, reveal the God of Love, and He is an ardent Lover. Our God is a consuming Fire. From its beginning at Baptism, the spark in the furnace is the God who is Love abiding in our souls as His home.

The soul who is House of God has space for God but also for other human beings. This house is not closed by shutters but has open windows. Light streams in, and there is dialogue with those outside. Still, there are secret chambers and inner rooms too, hidden to the outside, places of intimacy. From these radiate out our most meaningful interactions with others. All our acts bear something of that heat from the fireplace warming the house and from there extend out into the cold world. Act follows from being and each one being a dwelling place of the God of Love, our acts bear love to the world. Love flows in and out of a house of God.

In each of the letters that follow, House of God is connected to the Divine Indwelling, the soul's dwelling in the Trinity, and depths of the soul as a place of communion with other souls too. In the first select letters — to her sister Marguerite (L 113), to her fellow nun, Sr. Marie of the Trinity (L 114), and again to her sister Marguerite (L 239) — Elizabeth reflects on the Blessed Trinity dwelling in our souls. The next letters show her emphasis on not only God abiding in us but also our abiding in God — letters to Canon Isidore Angles (L 177) and to Canon Angles's sister-in-law (L 184). The final few letters touch on the fact that, when God dwells in our souls as His own house, others find a place in our heart too. Elizabeth speaks of a hidden rendezvous through faith with her loved ones in letters to her mother's friend and the mother of her friends — Madame de Sourdon (L 157), to Madame Gout de Bize, whose chocolate was the last thing she ate in the final days of her life (L 330), and to her friend Antoinette de Bobet (L 333).

God Abides in Us

The Trinity's abiding presence is central to St. Elizabeth's understanding of being a house of God. Carmelites receive a title with their religious name. For St. Thérèse it is *of the Infant Jesus and the Holy Face*. For Sr. Elizabeth it is *of the Trinity*. The feast of the Holy Trinity becomes her name day and she writes to her sister after she celebrates it as a Carmelite for the first time. She delights to spend the day buried in attentiveness to the presence of her Three under the mantle of silence and adoration. She is also struck by the meaning of her name, and in this letter written in 1902 she draws her sister into this mystery:

> *O yes, my Guite, this feast of the Three is truly mine. There is none other like it for me. It was a good one in Carmel, because it is a feast of silence and adoration. Never have I understood so deeply the Mystery and the whole vocation that my name has in it. I have entrusted you to the Three, my Guite, see how I establish you. Yes, I keep my rendezvous with you in this great Mystery. May He be our Center, our Abode.* (L 113)

St. Elizabeth loved her sister and would stay closely connected to her as the cloister permitted through visits, letters, and prayer for the rest of her life. As children, they studied more than piano together in their little apartment. Now, they study holiness. In her first year in the cloister of the Dijon Carmel, Elizabeth proposes to her sister Guite many of her own heart's desires and intuitions. As she comes to understand and live more perfect intimacy with her *Maestro*, she wants to share this with her sister. From early childhood, God began His work in them, filling their souls with a longing for intimacy with Him, a sensitivity to His presence, a love for His eucharistic presence, a deep awareness of His triune Personhood, and a strong desire to draw others into intimacy with God. From within the monastery's enclosure, through her prayers and letter writing, letters written from the heart, Sr. Elizabeth sought to bring many others into the depths of love's abyss, but none as much as Guite.

During the years she spent waiting to enter Carmel, after first perceiving God's call to her at age fourteen, Elizabeth sought to carry on with her daily activities while attending to God present in her interior abyss. She would enter into a solitude of spirit, a detachment from everything that was not God, by remaining in profound interior silence (HF 7). Now finally she is hidden away in Carmel's embrace and her silence grows within her simplicity of intention: she seeks only God and refers all things to Him (HF 21). Her *simplicity of intention* is likewise strengthened by interior silence. Together they serve her *abiding with the Three,* whose home she is. As Sr. Elizabeth of the Trinity, this is her very vocation. She will come to appreciate, even more fully, silence as an essential condition for such attentiveness, and ultimately for holiness. Before her death she wrote to her Carmelite sisters:

> *My Rule tells me "Your strength will be in silence." This means that to stay strong in the Lord, interior silence unifies one's whole being. Interior silence keeps all of one's powers occupied with the sole occupation of love. To be interiorly silent is to have "the focused" gaze which permits the light of God to illumine us.* (LR 3)

Silence allows for this work of love, the soul's gazing upon God in faith and simplicity. With that single eye, the simplicity of intention, Elizabeth allows God to *satiate within [her] His need to communicate "all that He is and all that He has"* (HF 43). Her adoration in the chapel of the Dijon Carmel on her feast is a magnificent expression of her soul's gazing with love upon the face of God. As a fruit of this gazing,

Elizabeth is drawn into the doctrinal Mystery of the Most Holy Trinity and into new depths in her relationship with her *beloved Three.*

Through the power, beauty, and thirst of His gaze, God communicates Himself to Elizabeth, and through Elizabeth His gaze is communicated to others and made fruitful in them. Her praise is directed toward Father, Son, and Holy Spirit and marked by sharing in the expansive radiance of trinitarian Love. Her praise of God goes out, so that, just as anyone who sees Jesus has seen the Father, so too anyone who sees Elizabeth sees the glory of the Trinity. This is the vocation in her name: to be House *of the Trinity. Of the Trinity* defines both the context of her silence and the object of her gaze. It is *in the Three* that Elizabeth establishes Guite as well. *May He be our Center and our Dwelling Place.*

Consumed in the One

All is lived in reference to the Father, Son, and Holy Spirit, and He is the context within which life unfolds. Here Elizabeth gives a beginning explanation of how to live focused upon, around, and within the Trinity. She instructs Guite in a prayer she learned from a Dominican Preacher, Père Vallee: *May the Holy Spirit carry you to the Word, may the Word guide you to the Father, and may you be consumed in the One.*

Elizabeth begins by drawing Guite into her own relationship with the Trinity. Guite will spend the rest of her life being brought deeper into this relationship. Drawn by the Spirit and inspired by Him, Elizabeth recognizes in God's Word a manual for holiness. Here Elizabeth encounters Christ, upon whom she gazes; in gazing she will be conformed to Christ and led to the Father, bringing others with her. *I'll rendezvous with you each day during the octave from noon to one o'clock.*

Elizabeth's noontime rendezvous with her sister for a common hour of adoration in thanksgiving and celebration of the feast of

Corpus Christi was a rendezvous under God's gaze. Although the two sisters did not sit shoulder-to-shoulder during this hour of adoration, as once they had done, Elizabeth knew that in the Spirit they were even more closely united now. Together they would allow God's eucharistic gaze to invite them into the silence "of the Trinity," where together they could be consumed by the love of the One — Father, Son, and Holy Spirit. Elizabeth shared with her sister her life of communion with her beloved Three.

In a personal relationship with each soul, God authors our pursuit of love. Love Himself is our beginning and end. And He is Himself the very love with which we are able to love and receive love to become love. St. Elizabeth invites us to rendezvous with her and to allow her instructions to serve as guideposts and inspiration for us in our journey toward greater intimacy with the Father, Son, and Holy Spirit, allowing God to be established as our center and our dwelling place. Like Guite, may we make Elizabeth's prayer our own prayer, for ourselves and all those God has entrusted to us: *May the Holy Spirit carry you to the Word, may the Word guide you to the Father, and may you be consumed in the One.*

On the same day that she encouraged her sister to pray for being *consumed in the One,* on the back of a holy card St. Elizabeth inscribes a similar thought to Sr. Mary of the Trinity, for whom the Trinity Sunday is also patronal feast: *In the depths of our souls, the One is consumed, with the Father, the Son and the Holy Spirit* (L 114).

With this short phrase, St. Elizabeth invites us to peer into the depths of a great mystery, a mystery of a vital communion. This is not a simple pious thought unreflectively proposed out of kindness. It is not the fruit of an effort to impress an elder. This prayer, instead, solemnly intends a new kind of solidarity that only God can accomplish. She is speaking into a deep spiritual hunger that haunts human existence: *God consumed in the depths of our souls.*

St. Elizabeth focuses on the inestimable gift of our faith. She is captivated by the God who has so lowered Himself that He has become our food! Notice that this spiritual food is not abstract or impersonal but profoundly relational — Father, Son, and Holy Spirit. In the Eucharist, we receive the incarnate Son, the Son in communion with the Father and the Holy Spirit. Only by consuming this Divine Personal Mystery of Communion can we find the sustenance we need to deal with the alienation that sin has caused in our soul. We are fed with the mystery of eternal connections and the exceeding immensity of love that the Divine Persons communicate.

We become what we consume. If we feed our hearts worldly things, we become worldly. If we seek to satisfy ourselves by that which merely delights our senses but does not allow our spirit to rest, ours will be at best a temporary and restless satisfaction. If we partake of what is above this world, we become heavenly even as we suffer the sorrows this world bestows. In Holy Communion, we consume God Himself through Jesus' Body and Blood, soul and divinity, truly present in the Blessed Sacrament. The Word-made-flesh offered for our sake renders the whole mystery of God food for the human heart. Because He has freely offered Himself as food, we must consume Him. Then He fills the vacant recesses of our hungry souls.

Our Father's House in the Center of the Soul

To her sister Guite, on August 13, 1905, she introduces a new dimension of House of God through a reference to the center of the soul, a teaching of St. John of the Cross. She makes a connection between the innermost center of the soul in the writings of her spiritual father with her own awareness of the soul as a kind of Heaven in which the Trinity dwells:

> *Oh! my Guite, Heaven, our Father's house, is in the "center of our soul"! St. John of the Cross will teach you that when we are in our soul's innermost center, we are in God. Isn't this both so simple and so consoling? Through everything, in the midst of your worries as a mother, even while dedicated to the little angels, you can withdraw into this solitude. Surrender yourself to the Holy Spirit so that He can transform you into God and imprint on your soul the Image of divine Beauty. In this way, the Father, tenderly leaning over you sees only His Christ and says: "This is my beloved daughter who delights me."* (L 239)

Elizabeth shares with her sister what she has been learning in her practice of prayer in Carmel. Guite, a young mother of two children, can herself enter into the same depths of prayer by entering into the depths of her soul where God dwells. Even in the midst of her duties in her household, she can turn inward and commune with the indwelling Trinity. The immediacy of God is greater than the immediacy of the world! It simply takes entering within, where God is more intimate to us than we are to ourselves. Elizabeth eloquently refers to this as *the invincible fortress of holy recollection ... the place of the "repose of the abyss" in which the praise of glory is called to abide* (LR 5, 7).

The invincible fortress of holy recollection is also an invincible fortress of truth, God's truth. It is the place of grasping anew by faith the truth of God and ourselves. It is a reawakening to the reality of God and who we are in God's eyes because of His work of salvation in Christ. In the depths of her soul, Guite is to discover the Father bending over her lovingly, as an adopted daughter in Christ, and saying, "This is my beloved daughter who delights Me" (see Matt. 3:17).

Earlier in the letter, Elizabeth shared with Guite some things from the Scriptures about our identity in Christ, *some wonderful things on the mystery of divine adoption ... to be children of God, my Guite, doesn't that excite you?* Elizabeth reveals she has been interiorizing some of the key scriptural passages to which she often returns, such as Ephesians 1:4–6 on God's eternal plan of predestination. This plan, for Elizabeth, is primarily not a far-off reality in the past or future, but a present reality being accomplished in the present moment and to be seized now by faith as a way to live and to be the person God created us to be.

Being rooted in our identity in Christ changes how we live. Christian morality requires primarily that we live out the new reality wrought in us through our divine adoption in Christ. We act in accord with our new name. Yet this reality is grasped now only through faith. By descending into the depths of our soul where God dwells, we come into living contact with our eternal destiny in Christ. In our interior abyss, where we are conformed to God in love, we encounter the indwelling Trinity, God imprints Himself in our soul, and we are transformed into His very likeness (L 335).

In interior recollection we are taken, for a time, from the multiplicity of external things and from the passing stimuli of time into an encounter the eternal God dwelling within. Things of the world often leave us scattered and dissipated. We can get caught up in the flux of superficial reactions of emotions, petty preferences, and personal opinions. We often act under the influence of the old man (see Eph. 4:22) of sin and egoism. To be drawn into the depths of our soul allows these superficial sentiments to pass away. Our mind, heart, and emotions can then be flooded with great interior silence and be reset, so to speak, as we return to our activities refreshed.

Yet there is more. Interior recollection can also be something of a rebirth. To return to the depths of our soul where the triune God dwells is to enter into contact with a more profound truth about ourselves in faith as wholly dependent on God and ordered to God. It is about reclaiming our identity in Christ. It is also living more profoundly the identity of our divine adoption, in prayer, where we are drawn more deeply into the life, light, and love of the Trinity. There we name Him our All — in adoration, surrender, and union. There is a spirit-to-spirit touch and tasting where the senses, imagination, and emotions remain on the outside. They are surely needed and can escort us there, but they must wait quietly outside the innermost sanctuary. Elizabeth says, *I am going to bury myself in the depths of my soul, that is, in God. Will you follow me in this very simple movement?* (L 239).

A simple movement: that captures it well. For it involves a gentle yielding to the subtle drawing of God from within. This requires simplicity of purpose and intention, but also simplicity of heart, mind, and soul, which all the external stimuli of the world can complicate. The external noise of the world can so easily drown out the silent music of God resonating out from our deepest center, where He dwells. Does this mean we have to practice prayer as if in a monastic cell of Carmel? At times it does require this. It also requires bringing this silent melody into the busyness of our day's activities.

There was an old custom in schools run by the Christian Brothers that at the chime of every new hour a voice would be heard over the loudspeaker, "Remember, you are in the holy presence of God." Elizabeth recommends something like this to her sister:

> *You might, in order to recollect yourself, every hour when you remember (or if you forget, it's fine), enter into the center of your soul where the Divine Guest dwells … It is said that St. Catherine of Siena always lived in a cell, even while in the midst of the world: that was because she lived in that inner dwelling place where my Guite too knows how to live!* (L 239)

Elizabeth recommends making one's whole life a prayer and also seeking periods of deeper prayer, dipping down into the abyss of our interiority at various moments throughout the day. We should take a moment's rest with God in our interior garden. It is about a quick glance at the faithful God who is Love itself, a quick thank you, a moment of adoration, a moment of delighting in His presence. If we forget at times to do this, Elizabeth insists that we should not be discouraged with ourselves, because it is more God's work of salvation in us than our own work. Instead, we must humbly surrender ourselves in trust and begin again. God's grace still goes before us and accompanies us even without our being aware. According to His eternal designs, God the Father continues to form us through the Holy Spirit into the beauty of His son as we press on in His grace with our daily tasks. Even then, our existence is unto the *praise of God's glorious grace.*

When we do remember to return to the center point of our soul to meet God anew, we are refreshed and reborn once again. At times we need to *return home,* recalling the House of God we are. In the midst of busyness or turbulence, we can enter deep within and be reborn, as all else is cleared away and we meet the living God at that interior point where His hand continually creates and recreates us. We often need to recommit ourselves to making the effort throughout the day to dip down into this interior abyss of intimacy with the Lord, whether at the chime of a new hour, when passing by a certain holy image, before or after certain tasks, or whenever struck with gratitude or a sense of great need. With practice, it can be done even in the midst of conversation and activity.

The more we love, the more we like to meet our beloved, even if for a moment. Like ourselves, Elizabeth so loves the Lord that she wishes to give Him her loving attention as much as she can as a house of God. In the end, this constant effort at attentiveness to her indwelling Beloved is part of her *Oblation to the Trinity*: *Pacify my soul. Make it Your heaven, Your beloved abode, and Your resting place. Let me never forsake You there, but may I be entirely present to You, taken up in my faith, wholly adoring, completely surrendered to Your creative Action.*

We Abide in God — an Ocean of Love

In writing to Canon Isidor Angles in 1903, a longtime family friend and confidant, St. Elizabeth offers an inverted perspective. She describes the mystery of God abiding in us in terms of how we abide in God:

> *I relish the thought that I left everything for Him. It is so good to give when you love, and I love so much this God who is jealous to have all of myself for Him. I feel so much love in my soul, it is like an ocean in which I immerse myself and lose myself: it is my vision on earth while awaiting the face-to-face in light. He is in me; I am in Him. It is enough for me to love Him, to let myself be loved, all the time, through all things: to wake up in Love, to move in Love, to sleep in Love, my soul in His Soul, my heart in His Heart, my eyes in His eyes, so that by His touch He may purify me, free me from my misery. If you only knew how He fills me.* (L 177)

Elizabeth is immersed in the Ocean of God's Love. God abides in her, and she also abides in Him. In God, as in an Ocean of Love, she abides and moves. Her language is reminiscent of St. Paul's words in the Areopagus of Athens, "In him we live and move and have our being" (Acts 17:28). Indeed, we live and move and have our being in the God who is Love.

This image of the Ocean of God's Love is a rich symbol of the life of contemplation: having periods of prayer, but also making one's whole life a prayer, as we are immersed in the Ocean of God's Love. The words Elizabeth uses to describe it give a sense of what contemplative prayer is for her. It is striking what she says about the *Ocean in which I immerse and lose myself. This is my vision on earth while awaiting the face-to-face in the light.* How could this immersion in God's love be something like a vision, a perception, a contemplative seeing through faith?

Initially, we can see the signs of God's love showered upon us throughout the day, from the most mundane to the most sublime, as manifesting something of God in His goodness, mercy, and fidelity. The testimony of such signs of His love gives us a spiritual vision of who God is. We know the One who dwells in our house. The household involves intimacy, but to be a house of God is not to contain the uncontainable as if to be master of it. How is it, then, that we can know this most Mysterious One? It is not a clear or distinct knowledge, but the experience of these many good things showered upon us by God that leaves us with a sense of God and His love. Our experience provides a spiritual vision or apprehension of God through the veil of faith that sustains us until the face-to-face vision in light.

The image of the Ocean of God's Love is still richer than this. It implies an even more direct contact with God. Elizabeth speaks explicitly of a *contact* with God and how much His Love *fills* her. This too yields a spiritual vision of sorts so she can say that immersion in the Ocean of God's Love *is my vision on earth while awaiting the face-to-face in the light.* How does this contact and being filled with God's love yield a spiritual vision or knowledge of God?

Consider an analogy. Does someone immersed in water have a certain knowledge of the water as it flows all around him? He is in contact with the water, he feels it, experiences it pressing upon him. It is a clear and elaborate conceptual knowledge of what water is, but especially as he drinks of the water and it *fills* him, this kind of knowledge of the water is all the more vital, especially if he is dying of thirst. The spiritual vision that this immersion in the Ocean of God's Love gives St. Elizabeth is like this. It is not a clear and elaborate conceptual knowledge of God but an intuitive, living knowledge of the Ocean of God's Love. She writes: *I feel so much love over my soul. He is in me, I am in Him. All I have to do is love Him, let myself be loved. So that, through His touch, He can purify me, free me from my misery. If you only knew how He fills me.*

Her vision or perception of God's love comes through being immersed and filled with God's love. She is surrounded and penetrated by the mystery of God. As a man immersed in the ocean knows water, so does Elizabeth know God. This is her spiritual vision in this life through the veil of faith, and it sustains her during her earthly sojourn. With this intuitive sense of the Lord — and the Ocean of Love that He is — Elizabeth's own love is able to expand to the further reaches of the Ocean of Love.

The Ocean of Love is expansive, binding souls together in its mystery. Earlier in her letter, Elizabeth reminds Canon Angles of a time he was present when her heart was taken up into God, *Up there, near the church, it was so beautiful in the silence and quiet of the night. Didn't you feel all my soul carried away to Him?*

Elizabeth's soul is carried away to God. She loses herself in the Ocean of God's Love. And she finds it so good to give when one loves, which ultimately means the complete gift of herself to God. It is only here, standing outside of herself, that she is granted this intuitive perception of the God who is Love. Her love stretches out and is in contact with God. Moreover, extending out beyond herself and giving of herself, she is attuned to God and His ways, God who likewise pours Himself out in love. Her house is set in order by the Divine Guest. Then, like knows like, *My soul in His Soul, my heart in His Heart, my eyes in His eyes.*

The union of love with God yields a secret, hidden perception of the God who is Love, even in this life. Her words about the beautiful evening near the church, now applied symbolically, provide the setting of this hidden exchange between the soul and the Divine Bridegroom. *It was so beautiful in the silence and quiet of the night.*

In the contemplative life, this calls for self-oblation. The immersion in God is brought about through a going-out of ourselves in a self-gift of love to God, even if only in the night. The *Oblation to the Trinity* of St. Elizabeth echoes some of these themes. *Immensity in which I lose myself.... Bury Yourself in me so that I may bury myself in You.*

Immersed or buried in the Ocean of God's Love, He buries Himself in us as we lose ourselves in His immensity. Here is a call to sacrificial love, in prayer and in our whole lives. It is a call to be surrendered, leaning back and floating on the Ocean of Love or yielding to its blessed undercurrents. In faith and hope we open ourselves to being drawn more deeply into the kind of loving contact with the Lord that Elizabeth describes, immersed in the Ocean of Love. Sometimes we will still see the shoreline; sometimes we will venture to the deep, to where we see and drink in only Love.

Abiding in Heaven, the House of the Father

On November 24, 1904, a week after the feast of St. Elizabeth of Hungary, Elizabeth of the Trinity writes the sister of Canon Isidore Angles and the aunt of a very close friend. In this letter that she entitles *My beloved is all mine, and I am all His,* she wants to provide encouragement. St. Elizabeth describes the role of the saints in helping us reach our heavenly homeland.

> *I am so touched by your kind wishes. As for me, I also honored you since Saint Elizabeth of Hungary is your patron. How helpful it is to see into the soul of the saints, and then to follow them by faith into Heaven. There they are completely luminous with the light of God. They contemplate in an eternal face to face! This Heaven of the saints, this is our homeland, this is the House of the Father where we are awaited, where we are loved,*

> *where one day we will ourselves fly away, and we will rest in the bosom of Infinite Love.* (L 184)

Forty-year-old Marie Angles, with the encouragement of her priest brother-in-law, entered the secular Third Order Franciscans. She took as her patroness St. Elizabeth of Hungary, another secular Third Order Franciscan who as queen devoted her life to good works. St. Elizabeth of the Trinity also looked to this queen as her patron, and on her November 17 feast day, this Carmelite remembered Marie Angles. She begins her letter expressing a special solidarity with her.

A few years before, Marie Metge had married Victor Angles, the brother of Isidore Angles, a Canon of Carcassonne. Madame Angles suffered from poor health and the couple were not able to have children. After Marie endured a painful and traumatic operation, Victor basically neglected her as she battled depression. She spent her days sitting alone on a lawn chair in an empty meadow while he distracted himself with work.

Through this difficult situation, the Lord was preparing her for a very special grace of conversion and prayer. Victor's brother, Canon Angles, began to meet with her and encouraged her to spiritual conversion. The isolation that once made her vulnerable to self-pity and misery became, through this priest's encouragement, an opportunity for deep prayer. Through continual silent prayer she learned to patiently bear her sufferings in a spirit of reparation until what had seemed meaningless became an opportunity for great spiritual fruitfulness. St. Elizabeth directs her message into this experience, with the purpose of encouraging her friend and helping to deepen the great grace that had begun in her life.

Elizabeth begins by providing a vantage point, the one place that allows a spiritual person to make sense out of the chaos of life: Heaven. Heaven is where we *rest* in the bosom of Infinite Love. It is where we are awaited. Moreover, it is where the saints are filled with the light that they contemplate *face-to-face*. What they see fills and transforms them. If we want to access our true homeland, we must follow the saints in faith. Their lives lead us to the *Father's House*. God abides in us as in His home but not as if we have domesticated Him or reduced Him to our own measure. God abides in us and we abide in Him. Accordingly, we have to adjust to dwelling not only in our own house but also in our Father's House. To enter this divine world we need to be expanded by faith.

To know something is to possess the truth of it. By its very nature, knowledge should purify our judgments about reality and intensify clarity about our lives. By faith we can possess the truth of Heaven, our true home, here and now in a way that will change our lives. By faith, all our judgments and decisions are ordered to a divine world that envelops us now *in this exile*. St. Elizabeth explains:

> *One sees the divine world already enveloping us in this present exile, a world in which we ourselves are able to move, oh, then, how the things here below disappear: everything that is, is not; it is less than nothing. The saints themselves have understood the true science, that which makes us leave everything, above all ourselves, in order for us to set sail in God and live only by Him!* (L 184)

Without faith, the world appears absolute. With faith, the world loses its absolute grip on us. Even when everything has fallen apart, in a world of broken dreams and broken hearts, the deepest truth is not the inadequacies and failures that we have suffered. Our weaknesses and limitations do not define who we are. God alone defines who we are. In all of our brokenness, the deepest truth is that God lives in us and we are in God. We set sail in Him on a journey beyond life's apparent failures, frustrations, and disappointments.

The more we see this, the more we know that we live for Him and not for this world. We are free from things and events and the claims they make on our existence. We live for something else, something from above, something more powerful than what we perceive by the natural light of reason. By faith, we have access to true knowledge — a true science — and we make ourselves open and vulnerable to this deeper, truer knowing when we enter into silent prayer. St. Elizabeth provides the reason that this is true, namely, Christ who dwells in us is working with great transforming power.

> *He is in us in order to sanctify us. Thus, we ask Him to be Himself our sanctity. When Our Lord was on earth, the Gospels witness, "hidden power came out of Him." By His touch, the sick were healed, the dead brought back to life. So it is: He is always alive! Alive in the tabernacle in His adorable Sacrament, alive in our souls. He Himself explains, "If anyone loves me, he will keep my word, and my Father will love him and we will come to him and make our dwelling in him." Thus, He is there. We keep Him company as the friend whom He loves! This is divine union and total intimacy, the very essence of our life in Carmel. This is what makes our solitude so dear, because as St. John of the Cross explains, "Two hearts in love prefer solitude above all else."* (L 184)

These words of encouragement divulge the great paradox of the Christian life: though we are set apart by God from the rest of the world, we are never really alone. In solitude, a greater solidarity awaits us. Some twenty-five years after this letter, Marie Angles will enter the Visitation at Orthez, consecrating herself with the name *Elizabeth-Marie*. Sr. Elizabeth of the Trinity had helped Marie find her life in God. Elizabeth left her mark on her older friend, helping make her another Elizabeth, that is, another house of God. St. Elizabeth wants to do the same for us.

Others Abide in Us in Love

Through the indwelling of the Trinity, a deeper solidarity with others opens up. The more we dwell in the Father's House, the deeper our unity with all those the Father entrusts to us. On February 21, 1903, St. Elizabeth writes to another friend's mother, Mrs. de Sourdon, who is very close to her family:

> *If only we knew how to be totally surrendered into the hands of our Father … I entrust your intentions to Him. Do not doubt Him. Abandon everything to Him as well as to me, your little friend. I will be your advocate. My mission is to pray without ceasing — and you know how true this is for you. I am so HAPPY with a bliss known by God alone. Resembling even the bliss of heaven, He is the Unique object of my happiness. During Lent, so divine in Carmel, my soul will be particularly united to yours. I will ask God to reveal to you the delights of His presence and to make your soul a sanctuary where He may come to be consoled. Will you permit me to enter deep into your soul and, with you, adore the One who abides there?* (L 157)

Elizabeth speaks here of her deep happiness in God. Saints are happy, and what is more, they want us to be happy too — not with a fleeting happiness or a transitory sense of peace, but with a deep and unearthly *bliss*. This is beatitude, a divine blessing, a surpassing joy that only God has the power to grasp. Yet, God the Father wills that we should share this secret bliss with Him, the bliss of possessing the Trinity, of being God's House, a place where He abides already in this life. Elizabeth asks to be able *to enter deep into your soul and, with you, adore the One who abides there*. It is worth recalling and taking St. Elizabeth at her word in her promise that she too is implicated in our happiness and life of prayer, and thus we should allow her to enter our hearts to teach us to love with even greater delight the Trinity who abides there.

In this communion of prayer and divine joy, as we hand ourselves over to Him, our souls are houses of God but also of others. *If only we knew how to be totally surrendered into the hands of our Father … I entrust your intentions to Him. Do not doubt Him. Abandon everything to Him as well as to me, your little friend. I will be your advocate.*

St. Elizabeth's words to her friend's mother, Madame de Sourdon, point to the first meaning of Christian prayer. The first movement of the prayer of faith is a humble cry for help, and behind this cry is trust that God can help. Cast before the tender mercy of God, this prayer brings to birth the first fruits of confidence in Christ Crucified. Our friends, united to us in prayer, strengthen this poor yet confident cry to God. *I will be your advocate,* Elizabeth promises. Yet, this first movement of prayer must grow from a transitory impassioned cry made in a moment of pain to a deeper and more abiding mystery. *I will ask God to reveal to you the delights of His presence and to make your soul a sanctuary where He may come to be consoled. Will you permit me to enter deep into your soul and, with you, adore the One who abides there?*

When St. Elizabeth says that she wants to *enter deep* into the soul of Madame de Sourdon, she is not expressing a sentimental or magical idea, but a conviction of faith. She is profoundly aware that God is present in her friend — not in a passive, static, ambiguous manner, but in an active, dynamic, and certain manner. Active, because God who is always at rest is always in act; dynamic, because His living presence evokes adoration and delightful love in those within whom He abides; and certain, because St. Elizabeth is convinced of the integrity of the faith of this longtime family friend, and even more, certain of the immensity of God's love for her soul. Is it possible for one soul to deeply enter another? Yes, in their mutually abiding in God, in their rendezvous in Him.

To be surrendered and to deliver oneself over to the Father is to find a resting place and home in God. This is where we find the other. If we are not completely surrendered to the Father, we are not only vulnerable to all kinds of anxiety and insecurity, but the deepest truth of our existence and destiny, that we are made for the communion of love, escapes us. We will remain enclosed in our own egotism, with life no more than a frantic grasp for control or a search for a nihilistic escape. We will remain shut off from God and neighbor. In our drive for achievement, we might have the house of our soul *swept clean and put in order*, but it will remain *vacant* with *the final state worse than the first*. With God reigning in the center of the House, however, we can drop our defenses and let the other in, without fear and in openness, as we turn together in joy to adore the God of Love who has called us all to Himself.

Abiding in the Furnace of Love

As God reigns, He is never passive. His love purifies and intensifies our whole being in a manner that anticipates the life of Heaven. In the Carmelite tradition, this divine action drawing us up into Heaven is described as fire, as a Furnace of love. On October 23, 1906, the dying Elizabeth writes to a special benefactor who has been supplying her chocolate bonbons, the only sustenance that she can take without getting sick. Madame Gout de Bize loves Elizabeth and has asked her to pray for her unmarried daughter Jaja's (Jeanne's) future. St. Elizabeth offers her one of her last letters in thanksgiving and friendship:

> *Be certain that on High, in the Furnace of love, I will be actively concerned for you. If you agree, I will ask on your behalf (and this will be the sign that I have entered Heaven) a grace of*

> *union, of intimacy with the Maestro. What has made my life an anticipated Heaven, I now confer on you — be convinced in every moment both day and night there is a Being called Love inviting us to live in union with Him. This means receiving equally every suffering as much as every joy, as coming directly from His love. This lifts the soul beyond everything that passes away, beyond all that wears it down. In such peace, in the manner of the love of the children of God, the soul finds its rest. Oh, dear Madame, how waves of tenderness swell in my heart toward yours.* (L 330)

Elizabeth's heart swelling with waves of tenderness is a dwelling place for God but also a shelter for her neighbor. There are implications of being alone with a God who is not just the Alone but *Infinite Solitude.* This is the beautiful and somewhat paradoxical name of God in Elizabeth's prayer to the Trinity: *Infinite Solitude.* It suggests an expansive solitude, not a self-enclosed aloneness; alone, yet expansive. Communion with a God in solitude means that Elizabeth's solitude also becomes infinite. Whereas initially solitude can feel confining, in the end, it reaches out into infinity when that solitude is spent in intimacy with the triune God. Elizabeth in the last stanza of her prayer exclaims, *My Three, my All, my Beatitude, Infinite Solitude, Immensity in which I lose myself!*

Elizabeth's solitude breaks out into infinity as her heart makes space to embrace others. It is not an uncommon experience for a time of solitude with God to deepen and enrich our communion with others. Truly, a soul that is a house of God is also a house for others. Elizabeth's solitude is expansive, enclosed with God alone while expanding to make room for everything in God's wide embrace. This infinite solitude takes her out of herself and enlarges her outreach and sphere of influence.

In her solitude, she is given a mission and purpose larger than herself, that encompasses the whole world. A house of God becomes a house for the world in its need for God. She tells Madame Gout de Bize that in Heaven she will be actively thinking of her and will win for her a grace of intimate union with God. Elizabeth anticipates that even in Heaven her heart will be turned toward others. Her promise to Madame echoes the heavenly mission she received precisely in an infinite solitude.

> *My mission in heaven will be to draw souls by helping them to go out of themselves in order to cling to God by a wholly simple and loving movement, and to keep them in this great silence within, which will allow God to communicate Himself to them and to transform them into Himself.* (L 335)

She lived her earthly life as an anticipated Heaven. She points Madame to the God dwelling within and this Divine Being is *a Being called Love*. In remaining alone with the Alone, she is alone with the Three, and they are Love. The Three are an outpouring of self-giving love in the unity of the one Divine Nature. The Trinity dwells in solitude but in a boundless solitude without confines. There is an outpouring of love in Their eternal processions, and there is a freely chosen outpouring of love in creation and redemption. This is the Being called Love who dwelt alone in Elizabeth's heart, creating a place for others in her heart as well.

When Elizabeth shares how her heart is moved with tenderness, she shares a childhood memory of strolling with her friend. *Little Elizabeth* wants to meet her there again. *Go recollect yourself on one of them and there, in under the gaze of God, you will feel her whole soul close to yours, for in Him we will be* one *for time and eternity!* (L 330).

The word *one* here is circled by Elizabeth in the original letter. Madame is to imagine being with Elizabeth in a familiar avenue, while *waves of tenderness* rise from Elizabeth's heart toward Madame's.

Perhaps the circled *one* is meant to convey that they are one in the Ocean of God's Love. The boundless ocean is a fine image of God and His infinity. God is Infinite Solitude as an Ocean of Love. And the outpouring of triune Love flows forth as waves of tender love flow out from Elizabeth's heart and her own infinite solitude. Elizabeth and Madame are *one* in that Ocean of Love. There is no need for Elizabeth to leave her solitude in embracing Madame, for both are contained in that Ocean of Love which is God, Infinite Solitude.

Love Alone Abides

In October 1906, St. Elizabeth writes to another family friend, M. Antoinette de Bobet.

> *Dearest Antoinette, only in the light of eternity does the soul see things rightly. Oh! how empty everything not done for God and with God is! I plead with you, seal everything with the mark of love! Only this abides. Life is something serious: every minute is meant to "establish" us more deeply in God… This is the secret: forget yourself, give up self, ignore self, focus on the Maestro, contemplate Him alone.* (L 333)

We all want to leave our mark on the world. This shows itself in big and small ways, from wanting to leave a legacy to carving one's initials into a tree. We want some lasting effect to remain from the passing vicissitudes of this life. We want our life to make a difference. St. Elizabeth shows us how to leave a lasting mark. *I plead with you, seal everything with the mark of love!* Every act made with love, marked by charity, echoes into eternity. It flows from God and returns to God and so has a lasting impact. Charity transforms the brief and fleeting bustle of passing tasks into acts of love that drive us further into the Eternal. In this way, every minute can truly *establish us more deeply in God.*

Love makes our faith radical in that it roots us deeper in God. This means that we draw our life from Him. His love allows us to mark everything with love. One obstacle to marking everything with love is our self-centeredness. Hence Elizabeth says, *This is the secret: forget yourself, give up self, ignore self, focus on the Maestro, contemplate Him alone.*

The human being reaches fulfillment only by looking away from himself toward *the other*. The human being, like all creatures, reaches his perfection only through something other than himself. Man's very being reflects this. Man has faculties that reach out beyond himself to the outside world. Through his five senses, he brings things into his soul for his intellect to ponder and his will to enjoy. As he brings good things into himself, from food and drink to spiritual goods, man is perfected. Man is fundamentally receptive to the good outside of himself. That is the great tragedy of self-centeredness. In greedily grasping and clinging to these goods, the self becomes the focus more than the good. This frustrates man's very being and purpose by turning him in on himself. It closes him off from *the other* and the good that really does perfect him. Having the self at the center turns man from the real to emptiness and illusion.

Real perfection, however, comes from being directed to *the other*, in receiving the good and doing the good in love. We see how Elizabeth's words strike at the very core of the human being: *Forget yourself, give up self, ignore self, focus on the Maestro, contemplate Him alone.... How empty everything not done for God and with God is!* In contrast, how full and substantial acts of charity done in God and marked by the eternal become. Gazing upon the Lord and stamping all our acts with love brings us to fulfillment and prefigures eternal life.

Elizabeth continues, *My beloved Antoinette, I leave you my faith in the presence of God. The God who is all Love and dwells in our souls. I bequeath to you this intimacy with Him "within." This has been the beautiful sun illuminating my life, making it already an anticipated Heaven.*

When *the other* that fulfills our being is God Himself, *the Other* is also more intimate to us than we are to ourselves. Otherness, gazing, activity, and union reach a new intimacy with the One who dwells within. Moreover, the *God who is All-Love* is Himself wholly directed to *the Other.* Father, Son, and Spirit dwell in an outpouring ecstasy of divine love and are completely turned toward one another in their communion of love.

Elizabeth's relational intimacy with God draws her out of herself into the same Other-directed stance of Father, Son, and Spirit in their sublime union of love. This illuminates her whole life as an anticipated Heaven. The eternal life of the communion of triune love begins to break into her earthly life. The three names that Elizabeth applies to herself — House of God, Praise of Glory, and Host of Praise — all bear that relational orientation to *the Other* so characteristic of Elizabeth's trinitarian spirituality and so much a part of humanity's destiny. She is a home for *the Other,* exists as His praise of glory, and is offered and handed over to *the Other* as His host of praise. In the light of eternity, Elizabeth has gleaned how all else save love is empty. She strives not to let time pass by in vain, but to root herself more deeply at every moment in the God who is All-Love.

Ongoing conversion very often is not so much a call to do different things but to do things differently. When our activities are suffused with love they are stamped with eternity and eternal life breaks into our world. The very same activities we were involved with before, now marked by love, bear the weight of eternal glory. This requires grace and a good bit of attention and effort on our part. St. Elizabeth's *Oblation to the Trinity* is ordered to this at least in part. Her life is offered as an oblation of *love* to the Trinity; every act flows from love and to love. She wants her whole life unto death to share in

Jesus' offering of love. To love like Jesus does, however, is impossible on her own. She needs Jesus to shine out from her. *I feel my weakness, and I ask you to "clothe me with yourself"* (L 335).

Elizabeth wishes Christ to shine out from her in all she does. Oriented away from self-centeredness and to Other-centeredness, she desires an interior recollection that is always attentive to the Beloved within, for whom she does everything. This vigilant attention to the Beloved derives from love and returns to love. Elizabeth wishes to bring this loving focus on the Other into all she does. Then all will be marked with the seal of love and her beloved Three. Because of the Three dwelling within her soul as House of God, everything changes.

CHAPTER TWO

PRAISE OF GLORY

ST. ELIZABETH'S MOST CELEBRATED name, Praise of Glory, involves her self-gift as directed to God in praise of His glory. Each of the reflections that follow touch on some aspect of being this praise of glory. Elizabeth not only praises God's glory in particular moments, but her whole being exists for the praise of His glory. She lives for the Other. She lives to radiate God's glory. Her message is that each person's identity and mission in Christ as House of God and Host of Praise are also to be radiant beauty as Praise of Glory.

To be a praise of glory implies a radical turning and orientation toward the divine Other. We are each called to this, and it ought to be lived out in a similarly radical turning toward our neighbor (L 191). Orientation to the other person — both divine and human — is captured in what could be called Elizabeth's personalism and indeed her tri-personalism. Her whole being as a praise of glory is ordered to the Father, Son, and Holy Spirit — the triune Persons whose very Being is constituted solely in being turned toward One Another, so the Son is who He is only in relation to the Father and the Spirit (L 269).

This personalism as a reflection of the Trinity requires the Christian to surrender himself to God in total gift to the other (L 298). To reach its fullness in this fallen world, often a self-gift made in the midst of suffering (L 311, L 312, L 314, L 315, and L 324) is necessary. Precisely in the weakness and poverty of suffering, God's power is made perfect and His glory is most evident. Since the glory we radiate belongs to God, becoming a perfect praise of glory most fundamentally involves letting ourselves be fully, deeply loved by Him and allowing His love to shine forth from our wounds and weakness to the great praise of His glory (L 337).

We will explore the praise of glory in relation to what we identify as trinitarian Personalism and the Other in L 191, L 269, and L 298. We also look at this same mystery in relation to self-gift and kenosis as radiating out God's love in L 311 and L 337.

Trinitarian Personalism and the Other

Elizabeth writes another letter to André Chevignard, this one on the feast of the Conversion of St. Paul in 1904. In it she quotes from Ephesians 2:19:

> *St. Paul says that "we are aliens or strangers no longer but belong to the City of the saints and the House of God." It is in that divine and supernatural realm, where we already live by faith, that my soul feels very close to yours in God's embrace, He who is all Love! His charity, His "exceeding charity," as the great apostle calls it, is my vision on earth. Will we ever understand how loved we are?* (L 191)

God's own exceeding charity — the great love with which we are loved (see Eph. 2:4) and joined together, one in the Lord, one in love — is the context and in a way the very truth of *everything* for Elizabeth. In this she echoes her *beloved St. Paul* who teaches that the knowledge of Christ's love surpasses all other knowledge and comes to us through faith, according to the riches of God's glory. A praise of glory shines forth from the center of this glory of Love: "the breadth and length and height and depth, and to know the love of Christ that surpasses knowledge, that you may be filled with all the fulness of God" (Eph. 3:18–19).

Elizabeth says this extraordinary, even excessive, charity is her own ideal on earth. For love of God she lives by faith, already now within the confines of her earthly life, like the saints worshipping before the throne of God's glory in Heaven. The Praise of Glory radiates God's exceeding love as she is herself caught up and overwhelmed by this love. Praise of Glory, St. Elizabeth's new name, gives expression to her practice of living Heaven by faith in all her daily activities. Received under God's inspiration just a few weeks earlier and referred to in this letter for the first time, here she exhorts the seminarian André Chevignard with St. Paul's words to the Ephesians, which express her new vocation-within-a-vocation. *Let us be "the praise of His glory."*

> *My soul loves to unite with yours in a shared prayer for the Church, for the diocese. Since Our Lord dwells in our souls, His prayer is ours and I would like to "communicate"* [literally, "receive Him," as with the Eucharist] *there unceasingly, remaining like a little vase at the Source, at the Fountain of life, to then give Him to souls, allowing the waves of infinite charity to flood them.* (L 191)

The Church is both mother of and home to this vocation of praise of glory and Elizabeth recognizes it as the vocation of all the baptized. She indicates it is nothing less than the universal call to holiness proposed by the Fathers of the Second Vatican Council. There is one holiness to which all are called, one participation in Divine Life, and St. Elizabeth specifies that this is the life of a praise of glory. Through these many praises of glory, united, sharing in Christ's own prayer to the Father, souls are drawn to God and *receive the flood of His infinite charity.*

It is a period of dramatic turmoil in the diocese of Dijon; many clergy and seminarians, distrustful of their bishop, are expressing rebellion and disobedience against him. It is a time when the bright message of God's love and grace is especially needed. In these circumstances Elizabeth invites Chevignard to join her in sharing in the movements of love of the Lord's own prayer. She allows herself to be made a conduit of God's *infinite charity* that this prayer draws down from the Father. She receives from God, and being filled, she makes herself a song of praise that communicates to other souls God's charity that possesses her. Elizabeth is a model for us of listening, receiving, sacrificing, praising, and adoring, revealing to us the dynamic of the life of a praise of glory.

We are freed for the silence and self-forgetfulness that are required to live as a praise of glory precisely by trusting in and docilely receiving the light of God's exceeding love. In receiving this love, we become holy with God's own holiness. Bound to God, His holiness bursts out from our soul into the world. Through her prayer, Elizabeth established herself, along with others, in God's love, and from the security of Love's fortress she was able to draw nearer to God and to receive Him into her soul with an increasingly perfect surrender. The Holy Trinity became her abode, her soul's home, when she turned her eyes to God and relinquished to Him her own preferences and concerns, and more dramatically still, any hostility toward Him. And gazing upon the exceeding love of her Three, she shines forth with the same love as a praise of glory.

Love demands a turning toward another, in delight and with concern for his good. The movement away from self, with its care for the other, is fruitful. In the relationship of love with God, the fruitfulness is manifest in the lover's own soul, in the Beloved's glory, and in the outpouring of love into other souls through God's glory and the lover's sanctity. Thus, in loving God we are made holy with His holiness, and the more we love Him, the more He is manifest to others through us. In Elizabeth's language, the lover becomes *a super-added humanity of Christ* as he or she is transformed by loving God.

Love makes possible what God demands of her — namely, total surrender — by Love and for Love. He unites her to Himself entirely and requires her all, but this gift magnifies His presence in her to others and His glory in creation. This is the life of the Praise of Glory. It is no surprise then that for Elizabeth there are two words that sum up all holiness and all apostolate: *union* and *love*.

This is to be fully alive and to *dwell completely hidden away in the Holy Trinity*. To be buried in Love's bosom is the longing of the lover's heart. "I found him whom my soul loves .... and would not let him go" (Song 3:4). And being buried there in Love's bosom as a praise of glory, we each radiate Love to others. *Will we ever understand how loved we are?* We will not. But as we pour ourselves out to the praise of God's glorious grace, this exceeding love of God transforms us and others through us.

An Illuminated Crystal

She writes to Guite at the end of April 1906:

> *When the veil is lifted, how happy I will be to disappear into the secret of His Face, and it is there that I will spend my eternity, in the bosom of the Trinity which was already my dwelling place on earth ... I leave you my devotion for the Three, to "Love." Live within with Them in the heaven of your soul. The Father will cover you with shadow, placing something like a cloud between you and the things of this earth to keep you all His. He will communicate His power to you so that you may love Him with a love as strong as death. The Word will imprint in your soul, as in a crystal, the image of His own beauty, so that you may be pure with His purity, luminous with His light. The*

> *Holy Spirit will transform you into a mysterious lyre, which, in silence, under His divine touch, will produce a magnificent hymn to Love; then you will be the "praise of His glory" that I have dreamed of being on earth.* (L 269)

Elizabeth describes the soul as a glittering crystal, sparkling with the beauty of the image of Christ, *pure with His purity, luminous with His light.* This is the task of the Praise of Glory. In this letter to her sister Marguerite (Guite), we understand that reflecting the glory of Christ is not just about blazing forth with the attributes of the Divine Being but has an utterly personal quality to it. We discover in this letter how radical Elizabeth's personalism truly is.

Her personalism is seen especially in the curious phrase *How happy I will be to disappear into the secret of His Face.* His face? We might have expected her to speak of disappearing into the secret of His presence, but no, it is *His Face* to which she refers. Prayer for this Carmelite is not so much about a contingent being coming into the presence of the Absolute Being, however sublime this may be. Prayer is coming before the face of God and disappearing into the secret of His face. The face of God conveys something about His Person. Elizabeth as Praise of Glory is not simply about the glory of God, but more exactly *the glory of God shining in the face of Christ.*

The idea of coming before the face of God is very biblical. The Old Testament has no word that corresponds directly to the English word *presence.* What is often rendered as "presence" in our English translations is more literally God's *face.* In Elizabeth's monastic *Manual of Prayers,* Psalm 31:21 is rendered more literally and that may be where she picked up this phrase. *You will hide them in the secret of your face against the mischief of the people.* The Old Testament's lack of the word *presence* is surely no shortcoming, for in its place is the wonderful theology of God's face. This implicit theology highlights the rich contours and character of the personal God. The God with a face has a history with His People. The great *I AM* is also the God of Abraham, Isaac, and Jacob. The theology of God's face also highlights the blessings and bright glory that shine forth from Him in His self-manifestation to us. In both the Old Testament and in rabbinic literature, we live because God's face gazes on us. Because the Lord looks at us and turns His face toward us we live, and we are filled with His blessings and intimate knowledge of Him.

What we would call being in the presence of God the Old Testament describes as being before the face of God. The intimate, personal love of God comes to the fore here, as it does in Elizabeth's words about disappearing into the secret of *His Face*. One's self-oblation to the Trinity culminates in entering into that hidden sanctuary of the exchange of personal love, *to disappear into the secret of His face.* Reflecting in prayer on being in God's presence should call to mind His face, radiant with all the richness and contours of His personal Being. God's presence is not just the weight of God's immensity, but also His face shining upon us with His personal love.

Even when Elizabeth speaks of Love, she highlights the personal. She tells her sister, *I leave you my devotion for the Three, to Love.* What is Love for St. Elizabeth? Rather, who is Love for her? Love is simply the Three, God All-Love, the Three Persons of the Trinity in personal communion.

The distinctness of the Three Persons is important for Elizabeth because she wants to enter into relationship with each of the Three. *Person* originally designated the mask worn by actors in ancient Rome. Does not the notion of the mask stand close to that of face? Face is in fact the more profound reality as it takes up what is meant by mask but with a new depth that corresponds to and reveals the inner being of the person. Elizabeth wants to *disappear into the secret of His Face.* In fact, it is the faces of Three she encounters, highlighting the distinction of the Persons in the unity of the Divine Nature.

Silence in prayer is seen by Elizabeth within this personalist context. Why silence in prayer? We could think of such reasons as: to bring to silence all that is not of God, to bring to rest and stillness to our wandering minds and hearts, and to empty ourselves to make room for God, but here Elizabeth highlights what silence is ordered to. Silence makes the soul a mysterious lyre, sensitive to every touch of God, producing a magnificent song in praise of God. Silence is about listening, entering into full, harmonious receptivity to God and His ways, being a reflection of His face. We saw that Mary's *fiat* brought her into full correspondence with God as a praise of His glory; we are invited to the same. Toward the end of the letter Elizabeth says that she will pray for Guite's little ones; but instead of assuring them that they would feel the effect of her prayers, she speaks of her personal presence. *Teach the little ones to live under the gaze of the Maestro. I would like for Sabeth to have my devotion to the Three. I will be at their First Communions. I will help you prepare them.* As she encourages her sister to teach the children *to live under the gaze of the Maestro,* that is, to live under the gaze of *His Face,* Elizabeth promises that she herself, in effect, will turn her face to her loved ones as she exerts her personal influence over them in the hidden workings of grace.

If for Elizabeth Love is simply the Three — the Three Persons of the Trinity in personal communion — it is no surprise that Elizabeth's love expresses itself as a personal communion. She will not only pray for them but *remain* with them. As a praise of glory before God's face, her radiating of His glory involves her face, her personal presence. In this she is simply radiating in complete harmony, as a mysterious lyre, the Love which is the Three.

Elizabeth loves best by dwelling in communion with the Three and extending this communion of Love to others. Her closing words capture something of all this. *A Dieu, little sister, I love you so much.... Whether in Heaven or on earth, we must live in Love to glorify Love!* More intimate communion with others comes by living more intimately with the Father, Son, and Spirit. *We must live in Love to glorify Love.* We must live in the Three Persons to be a praise of glory and show Love's face to others.

My vocation is love

To be a praise of glory of the God who is all Love requires Elizabeth to place herself in Love. *My vocation is love.* This letter to Marguerite is filled with loving instruction about the *secrets* of Elizabeth's vocation of love, and is yet another testament to the extraordinary love shared by these two sisters. The letter is written on the great feast of the Carmelites, Our Lady of Mount Carmel. Elizabeth's recently renewed personal devotion to the Holy Virgin causes her to entrust Guite and her daughters to Mary, Queen and Guardian of Heaven. Elizabeth seeks to draw Guite into the work God is doing in her own soul advising her:

> *You must erase the word "discouragement" from your vocabulary of love; the more you feel your weakness, have difficulty in recollecting yourself, and the more hidden the Maestro seems, the more you must rejoice, because it is then that you give to Him. In love isn't it better to give than to receive? God told to St. Paul: "My grace is sufficient for you, for power is made perfect in weakness," and ... he exclaimed: "I boast of my infirmities, for when I am weak, the power of Jesus Christ dwells in me." What difference does it make how we feel? God, He is the Immutable, He who never changes: He loves you today as He loved you yesterday and as He will love you tomorrow. Even*

> *if you have caused Him suffering, remember that abyss calls to abyss and that the abyss of your misery, little Guite, attracts the abyss of His mercy. He helps me understand that for both of us.* (L 298)

Like she did for Guite, Elizabeth wants to share with us her understanding of what God desires. Even though our vocation to love is beyond our own ability, because it has been entrusted to us and not simply chosen by us, we ought to surrender with our will, crying, *Fiat!* It is God's own Love that is the foundation, the impetus, the context, the force, and the end of our effort to love. We are the praise, not of our own glory, but of His glory. We need only to make ourselves docile in an act of surrender to Love. Then Love Himself will make our docility powerfully fruitful. He will draw us into the depths where He dwells, so that we, abiding in His silence, receive His love into the deepest recesses of our being.

By beginning with this spiritual truth, there is nothing Elizabeth could propose that would remain beyond our grasp. It is precisely our weakness and incapacity that attracts God's mercy and enables us to *live Love*. God Himself will accomplish His Divine Will in us because we allow Him to make up for our lack, strengthen our weakness, and forgive our sins and failures.

Docile surrender to Him in our life's circumstances becomes our gift of self to others. At this point in her life, Elizabeth's days and nights unfold against a background of suffering. Suffering, then, is her place of encounter with the Lord. Her trust in His love and her willed decision to relinquish her own preferences carry her beyond her feelings and a natural abhorrence of physical suffering. She chooses to allow God to make her circumstances an occasion of more perfect conformity to Christ in His sufferings and Passion.

Obviously Guite's life circumstances were quite different from Elizabeth's. As a young wife and mother of two little girls, Guite's offering was fashioned out of the demands on her time and energy as well as of her sorrow for her dear sister's imminent death. Guite's suffering in her sacrifices was very different from Elizabeth's calvary. Yet, like Elizabeth, Guite gave love in the way God invited her to. Elizabeth recognized that the road descending into the Abyss of Mercy opened out before both of them, all of its particular twists and turns made into occasions of conformity to God's will according to each one's circumstances. *The gift of self: it seems to me that this is the consummation of love. Little sister, do not squander any sacrifice, so much can be gathered up in a day. With the little ones you have many occasions … give everything to the Maestro. Don't you find that suffering unites us more perfectly to Him?* (L 298).

The gift of self is the *consummation of love*. The personal gift of self makes us most like God and radiates the glory of God's love. The suffering that often accompanies the gift of self, our death to our plans and preferences, to our desires, and ultimately even to our very sense of self, our self-identity, can act as a spark, igniting a fiery passion in our loving. It can intensify our desire for God. Our increased desire fans the flame of God's love burning in us and moves us to allow Him to consume us as we share in His love for our neighbor. When we unite our sufferings to His in obedience to His will, we gift Him and others through our participation in Christ's own obedience in His Passion.

The royal road of suffering is familiar to saints and holy souls. About it, Elizabeth writes to Guite in an earlier letter (L 269): *If you have to suffer, think that you are even more loved.* It is the same road upon which Jesus lived the life of a praise of glory embracing the Father's will patiently and gratefully, no matter the cost.

> *I must ceaselessly immolate myself so as to be conformed to my crucified Bridegroom ... This is that mystical death in which the soul annihilates herself and so completely forgets herself that she goes to die in God so that she might be transformed into Him ... this requires suffering, for all that is in us must be destroyed in order for God to replace it with Himself.* (L 298)

But again, this *destruction, annihilation,* and *death,* in the mysterious paradox of glory, leads to the fullness of eternal life, the luminosity of Truth's Light, and an expansive share in the excessive love of God's own Self-Gift. Elizabeth, Praise of Glory, draws closer to the culmination of her vocation as love by drawing other souls into her hymn of love — implanting in them her own love for God (L 288). She trusts God to reciprocate in her soul by rooting His love in her so that it might emanate through her to others. *I love to share these things with you, little sister, echo of my soul ... carrying you above what is finite, into the bosom of Infinite Love ... my soul overflows tonight, for I feel my Maestro's "excessive love" and I would like to place my soul in yours so you would always know this love, especially in your sorrows* (L 298).

Elizabeth's passionate heart desires to include Guite in the ardor of its love so that Guite might share her sister's joy at the prospect of resting in the Father's Heart. Elizabeth's hope is also for us, that we will associate ourselves with her by being conformed to Christ in His work of adoration, reparation, and salvation, each as a praise of glory. God's gift to us of our life, fruit of His love, is gifted back to Him for His glory by bringing *everything* into *Light, Love, Life.* Then, all that will show forth from us will be His light, love, life, our conformity having been accomplished.

Where Did Christ Dwell if Not in Suffering?

— St. Angela of Foligno

During the final weeks of Elizabeth's personal passion, she came across this quote of St. Angela of Foligno in a volume of her writings that was given to Elizabeth by her mother at Mother Germaine's request. A few days later, on the feast of the Exaltation of the Cross, Elizabeth wrote to Guite that she had found her dwelling place in the Lord's immense suffering. *He is this dwelling place, [Christ] Himself, the Man of Sorrows* (L 311).

Elizabeth's own understanding of suffering and her desire to be conformed to Christ Crucified found a certain approbation and consolation in these words of this great Italian mystic. Angela of Foligno recognized the sufferings of the Crucified God-Man as His supreme act of love, conforming and transforming souls through love. Conformity to Christ, the vocation of a praise of glory, Elizabeth's vocation within a vocation, was to be realized through her suffering in love, especially as she drew near to the end of her life.

Christ as *the perfect Praise of Glory* is the perfect glorification of Love through His suffering even unto death on the Cross. In the face of betrayal He says, "Now is the Son of man glorified, and in him God is glorified" (John 13:31). And in reference to His Cross, He says, "What shall I say, 'Father save me from this hour'? No, for this purpose I have come to this hour. Father, glorify thy name" (John 12:27–28). Like for the Crucified, suffering becomes an invitation to glorify God.

Elizabeth's life was so deeply marked by physical suffering at this point that here in Letter 311 she refers to herself as a chalice and reminds her sister that saints are made according to their love for the Cross. By dwelling with Christ in His suffering, she surrenders herself to the Cross' demand for her all. She surrenders her whole being in acts of love for God and souls. Her extreme suffering finds satisfaction in its power to further conform her to her beloved Crucified so that she might become a *radiating* of the glory of God's love.

Repeatedly Elizabeth counseled those dear to her to allow Christ to conform them as well. She emphasized this as a shared conformity with Mary, the Mother of Sorrows, to her son, the Man of Sorrows. To a friend who was grieving the loss of her daughter she wrote:

> *It is by way of the pierced heart of the Mother of Sorrows that I come to you. You have consummated your sacrifice ... I am begging that Mother to fill your soul with the same peaceful serenity and vigor that marked her in her own bitter martyrdom. Referring to the Maestro, one saint asked: "Where did He dwell but in suffering?" Every soul buried in suffering dwells with Him; she remains united with Jesus Christ in His immense suffering of which the prophet sang; Saint Paul calls this the dwelling place of the predestined — those whom the Father "foreknew and predestined to be conformed to the image of His Son, the Crucified."* (L 312)

St. Angela confirmed for Elizabeth that her call to be a praise of glory is realized in her great physical sufferings which conform her to the Crucified One. This call to dwell in the Lord's suffering with Him is a development of Elizabeth's understanding of that predestination-in-love that she encountered in the writings of St. Paul and to which she repeatedly refers. The image of the Son to which we have been predestined to be conformed according to Romans 8:29 is, for Elizabeth, precisely the image of *the One crucified by Love* (LR 1; cf. L 324). She even adapts the verse from Romans to reference the Crucified One.

> *Living in continuous contact with God, we see everything by His light, the only true light. In this light it is revealed to us that every form of suffering is God's greatest pledge of love for His creature. As St. Paul writes, those whom the Father foreknew and predestined He conformed to the image of His Son, the Crucified.* (L 315)

Herself buried in profound suffering, Elizabeth encourages her spiritual children to live each moment as an unceasing praise of glory, abiding in prayer with Jesus on the Cross, and entering into the *repose of the abyss* through contemplation of *God crucified by love* (L 314). Elizabeth's contemplation opens her to receive the gift of conformity to the Son in His Crucifixion by means of her own, so to speak, crucifixion. She recognizes in this divine gesture of association an expression of God's love for her. She receives her suffering as God's love bestowed and she returns to Him her poverty-in-suffering. Once again, she allows herself to be made to resemble Christ through her prayerful, love-filled surrender to the Father's will for her.

> *Never before had God made me realize so clearly that suffering is His greatest promise of love to His creature. Do you see, at each new suffering I kiss the Maestro, thanking Him: "I am not worthy." I think of suffering, His life's companion, I do not deserve the same regard from the Father as He received. One saint wrote in speaking of Jesus Christ: "Where then, did He dwell if not in suffering?" David sang that this suffering was as vast as the ocean. All souls crushed by suffering of any kind can exclaim: I live in intimacy with Jesus Christ, we dwell together in the same home!... We can recognize that God is dwelling within us and that His love has taken possession of us if we receive everything which wounds us or causes us suffering with patience and gratitude ... It is necessary to contemplate God crucified by love. Contemplation that is true unfailingly leads the soul to love of suffering.* (L 314)

Suffering becomes a refuge for Elizabeth, a dwelling place of intimacy with her Beloved. Intimacy with the Beloved gives her suffering meaning and transforms it into acts of love. Contemplation of the Crucified brings her here. Elizabeth is not advocating for suffering for its own sake but recognizes that the intimacy with the Beloved that she seeks is hidden in the depths of her suffering.

This breathtaking spiritual lesson, so reminiscent of the teaching of her Carmelite father, St. John of the Cross, is given on the heels of a word to her mother about the particulars of a warm petticoat she has requested. Elizabeth remains *in the world,* affirming the kindness of her mother's maternal concern, but not *of the world,* so powerfully evidenced by her exhortation.

Elizabeth desires this for us, and she makes her invitation to live as a praise of glory clear and simple. *Every trial, annoyance, and lack of courtesy must be accepted in the Cross' bright illumination. In this way we can please God and progress in the science of love.* Here is Elizabeth's path to conformity with the Crucified. As she learns to look at life from God's perspective, by the light of the Cross, Elizabeth discovers that her happiness *intensifies in proportion to her suffering* (L 315). She continues to practice *quotidie morior,* dying-to-self, and fixes her gaze on the Father, on the secret of His face. She joins herself to others in their sufferings as she draws them into Christ's Self-Offering on the Cross, making Him present to them in their sufferings.

> *Without a doubt we naturally feel anguish in the face of suffering — the Maestro willed to know this humiliation — but the will must learn to dominate all feelings and say to the Father in Heaven: "Thy will be done and not mine." Speaking of Christ, one saint said: "Where did He dwell if not in suffering?" Every soul that suffers dwells, therefore, with Him. I rendezvous with you in that dwelling place.* (L 315)

Elizabeth also continues to develop her understanding and explanation of the *rendezvous*. In this letter to an old friend, she establishes her invitation to *rendezvous* in a shared participation in Christ's own suffering. Elizabeth's docile receptivity to the Father's will, so that it might be fully accomplished in her soul, has the real consequence of keeping her close to Him in the abyss of His love. The Crucified is embracing her, and she wants all those *predestined by divine election* to join her in Love's embrace.

> *Little sister of my soul, in light of eternity God makes me understand some things more clearly and I tell you as if this were His word, do not be afraid of sacrifice, of struggle, but rather, rejoice! If it is in your nature to be combative, [you are] like a battleground, do not be discouraged or sad. I lovingly encourage you: love your misery, because it is into our misery that God extends His mercy and when you are overcome by sadness and withdraw into yourself, that is self-love! When you fail, hide yourself in your Maestro's prayer. Yes, little sister, from His Cross He saw you and prayed for you, and His prayer is eternally living and present before His Father. It is that prayer which will save you from your misery. The more you feel your own weakness, the greater your confidence must grow, because it is upon Him alone that you must lean.* (L 324)

That feeling of being overwhelmed with an awareness of our own weakness, an all-too-familiar sentiment for many of us, is precisely the point of entry into the Praise of Glory's renunciation of self and of all pretenses of control and worthiness. Again, we are a praise, not of our own glory, but of His glory. The greater our poverty, the weaker we discover ourselves, the more we can expect that God desires to be glorified in us, and to the degree that we choose to give Him free reign.

Elizabeth wants her message to be received into our hearts as from God directly. Liberation, transformation, and ultimately divinization lie buried in His embrace of mercy, to which we have access by hiding ourselves in Jesus. We will be made by Love into love. In our own being we will become mercy to others as we allow Christ's cries to the Father on our behalf to become our own cries to the Father on behalf of others. In this way, we will give great glory to God by resembling His beloved son who wills to make us true praises of glory, the glory of triune Love. Your life as praise of glory begins now in your joys and sufferings, both great and small. Your self-gift is an offering of your life, as you are right now, in your particular circumstances.

Let Yourself Be Loved

This letter, so much more than simply a farewell note, is recognized as one of Elizabeth's major works: *Let Yourself Be Loved* (L 337 is LL). Addressed to Mother Germaine, it remained hidden from everyone but Mother herself until after her own death years later, when it was found amongst her papers, although Mother had occasionally mentioned it to the other sisters. In this very personal message, Elizabeth unveils the inner dynamic of the Praise of Glory. She reveals that receiving Love is the center of praise. The call is simply to let ourselves be loved and, receiving the Lord's love, to live by drawing from and pouring out love with bold and confident trust. In an earlier letter to her mother, Elizabeth likened herself to the Host offered at Mass and shared her *secret* to living Heaven on earth by faith (L 309). She is a praise of glory to the extent that she is a host-victim (*hostie*). Here at the end of Elizabeth's life, the Father's will is manifest to her through physical sufferings and the limitations they impose on her within the context of the obligations and expressions of her life as a Carmelite.

Hers is a call to surrender everything, even her very life, into Love's immense furnace. She is to be a praise of glory as a sacrifice of praise. Ultimately a praise of glory becomes a host of praise.

Elizabeth's surrender to perfect conformity, now nearly accomplished, frees and emboldens her to encourage Mother Germaine, saying, *Listen to [me] as if to God's "spokesperson"* (LL 1).

Elizabeth bequeaths to Mother Germaine her vocation as praise of glory in a way especially suited to Mother. Elizabeth insists that Mother Germaine is preferentially loved by God, and she needs to accept this truth, heedless of the obstacle of her weakness.

> "You are uncommonly loved," *loved by that preferential love that the Lord had for some here on earth and which carried them so far.... Listen to His word to you:* "Consent *to being loved, even more than these! Do not fear that any difficulty would be an obstacle, for I am free to lavish My love on whomever I want!* 'Allow *yourself to be loved more than these'* is *your vocation; it is by being faithful to it that you will make Me happy, because in this way you magnify the power of My love. This love can restore anything you could destroy."* "Let *yourself to be loved more than these."* (LL 2, L 337)

The accent in Elizabeth's message to Mother Germaine is on receiving, on allowing herself to be loved. Our failures and weaknesses are not a hindrance to being a praise of glory. For God's merciful love is glorified precisely *through* our weakness and neediness as we receive His love in utter trust and docile surrender. Elizabeth speaks to her Mother Superior with the authority received on account of Elizabeth's total abandonment to the Father's will. The audacious courage required of Elizabeth, so she can deliver God's word to her superior, is born of love. This too is a key element in the interior dynamic of being a praise of glory — to receive God's love and allow it to become a source of love which breaks forth in a boldness of faith for Love's sake. Elizabeth draws from Love by whom she has been loved and trusts in the workings of God's grace as she extends God's call of beloved-ness to Mother.

Elizabeth offers herself for Mother and unites her to her own heavenly existence (as anticipated in her letter). Elizabeth exhorts Mother to dwell alongside her in Heaven while still living here on earth, by abandoning herself in receptivity to God's love. This is Mother Germaine's particular life in praise of glory—to abandon her fears about her own failures and weaknesses and to fully surrender herself to Love, recognizing God's special desire for her and allowing herself to be caught up into the life of Heaven.

> *Dearest Mother, spend your life in Heaven where I will be singing the eternal* Sanctus *in your name: I will not do anything before God's throne without you … I will come and live in you. Now it is my turn to be your little Mother. I will teach you, so that my vision will benefit you, so that you might share in it, and so that you may also live the life of the blessed!* (LL 4)

Elizabeth, Host of Praise, perseveres in her apostolic self-offering to the very end, spreading God's love by word and deed. In fact, her *mission from heaven* (L 335) testifies to her desire to live for others even after her death. The context of love within which she has sought to receive and be formed in her vocation now becomes the content of her prophetic word to Mother Germaine and the particular *unum necessarium* of Mother's own vocation as a praise of glory.

> *I entrust to you this vocation that was mine in the heart of the Church Militant and which from now on I will ceaselessly fulfill in the Church Triumphant:* "Praise of Glory of the Holy Trinity." *Mother, "let yourself be loved more than these": this is how your Maestro wills for you to be a praise of glory! He rejoices for you to be built up by His love and for His glory and He alone wants to work in you, even though you have done nothing to attract this grace besides your creaturely works of sin and misery … This is how He loves you. He loves you "more*

> *than these." He will do everything in you; He will love to the end, because when a soul is so beloved to Him in this way, with an unchanging and creative love, a love that is free to transform according to His purpose, what progress this soul will make!*
>
> *Mother, the Maestro asks you to keep company with Love, and to flow into and root yourself in this Love who wants to sign your soul with the seal of His power and His grandeur. You will never be insignificant if you are vigilant in love!* (LL 6)

Through a divine inspiration, Elizabeth understands that Mother Germaine needs to let herself be loved by the Lord. Elizabeth recognizes that greater confidence in God's love will release His transformative power in Mother. If she allows herself to be loved like this, *What progress her soul will make!* (LL 5).

A praise of glory must *know and believe in the love God has for us*, for *we love because He first loved us*. This is a call to a simpler trust in God's love, which in turn will allow the Praise of Glory to reflect the perfect simplicity of God's love. According to Elizabeth, this message addressed to Mother, filled with the forceful power of a divine word, is Love's promise to Mother Germaine.

> *You will never be commonplace if you are attentive to love! But at those times when you feel only desolation and weariness, you will please Him if you faithfully* believe *that He continues to work, that He loves you the same, and* even more*: because His love is* free *and this is how He desires to* magnify Himself *in you; and you will* allow *yourself be loved* "more *than these." This, I believe, is what it means to ... Live in the depth of your soul! My Maestro makes me clearly understand that He wants to do glorious things: you are called to render homage to the simplicity of the Divine Being and to magnify the power of His Love.* (LL 6)

Simple trust in God's love magnifies the simplicity of the Divine Being who is All-Love. Elizabeth concludes her letter asking Mother Germaine one more time to receive these words as coming from God Himself. She then quotes the Lord's words to St. Angela of Foligno, words which are also meant for Mother Germaine: *I will accomplish great things in you; in you I will be made known, glorified, and praised* (LL 7). In receiving Love, the soul will be a place where God is known, glorified, and praised. By letting herself be loved, the soul will be a praise of God's glory.

Receiving God's love and walking boldly in faith extends God's love to others. In this letter Elizabeth has unveiled the inner dynamism of being a praise of glory. By letting ourselves be loved in simplicity of heart, we live out of bold trust in this Love, becoming a praise of God's glory. Elizabeth's repeated emphasis on a recollected simplicity can help us put this into practice. When we fix our gaze in all simplicity on God's love and His purposes, setting aside our useless doubts and fears, we will come to live our particular call to be the praise of His glory.

Through Elizabeth's words, God addresses His word to us as well, a word intended for *us* in *our* particular circumstances, a word of Love to build us up. Rooted in our identity as House of God, Praise of Glory, and Host of Praise, we open ourselves to receive God's love and, in turn, *live the truth,* acting from the gift we have received. With this letter, Elizabeth conveys God's appeal as directed to us as well. When we entrust ourselves in simplicity to God All-Love and allow Him to define the contours of our life, then we can live out of our trust in the power of His love for us and for others. We need to receive His love into the depths of our being and submit to its claim on us and on *everything* in our life — relationships, decision-making, time, money, attention, sins, addictions, attachments, weaknesses, and even our efforts in acquiring virtue.

As we allow Love to heal us, to fill us, and to overflow from us, we will truly become a praise of His glory.

In her soul's heaven, the praise of glory has already begun her eternity's work. In her uninterrupted song she is under the power of the Holy Spirit who effects everything in her. Though she may be unaware of it, the weakness of nature preventing her from being attentive in God without distractions, she always sings and she always adores, for she has given herself entirely to praise and love, so great is her passion to give glory to God. In the heaven of our soul may we become praises of glory of the Holy Trinity and praises of love of our Immaculate Mother. Someday the veil will be lifted and we will be brought into the eternal courts where we will sing in the bosom of Infinite Love. God will give us "the new name promised to the Victor." What will it be? *LAUDEM GLORIAE.* (HF 44)

CHAPTER THREE
Host of Praise

St. Elizabeth of the Trinity, House of God and Praise of Glory, also becomes Host of Praise. A host (or victim) of praise is something that is consumed. It is a holocaust, a whole burnt offering. When we hear the phrase *for the greater glory of God,* we tend to be spurred on to do greater things for the glory of God. There is an essential place for this holy effort of love, but in the Praise of Glory becoming Host of Praise, the emphasis is on being offered and consumed. There is love sacrificing but there is also love sacrificed, which is about accepting the painful unfolding events of life, through which the old self dies and we are offered as an oblation to God. We surrender and give our *fiat* as a host of praise in trust-filled self-abandonment. Then, as the holocaust is completely consumed, the Host of Praise passes over into the next life, completely given over to her beloved Three.

This oblation of the host, or victim, of praise has value because it is accomplished in union with the redeeming work of Jesus Christ and His self-offering as a Victim of Praise on the Cross. Jesus is first and foremost the Host of Praise. Elizabeth's self-oblation conforms her to the redemptive offering of Jesus, especially as it is perpetuated daily in the Holy Sacrifice of the Mass. As Host of Praise, she unites herself to Jesus in the Host offered in the Mass. For Elizabeth, the name Host of Praise has a clear connection to the eucharistic Host. The context of her oblation is liturgical and sacramental.

Elizabeth's offering as Host of Praise has its foundation, source, model, strength, and perfection in the Lord Jesus' offering in the Holy Eucharist. It is precisely here that she seeks conformity — in Christ's eucharistic self-offering. Letter 244, L 165, and L 256 are addressed to a seminarian and a priest, but indeed, Elizabeth recognizes that to be a host of praise is the call of all Christians. We must keep our eyes fixed on the things of faith in order to be drawn into the dynamic of the Son's self-giving love in the Paschal Mystery. This theme is considered in L 288 to her sister and in L 324 to her friend Germaine de Gemeaux. Letter 291 and L 309 show how the meaning of Host of Praise involves a life of love, as desire and surrender, and ultimately a trusting self-abandonment into the hands of God. Trustful surrender is the daily bread of a host of praise.

Rooted in Jesus' Eucharistic Self-Offering

Elizabeth starts her letter to Fr. André Chevignard with a quote from Philippians 3:20, *Our life is in heaven* (L 244). The life of Heaven is always before Elizabeth, beckoning to her. Her great longing is to be caught up into the life of the Trinity. She prays, *Bury Yourself in me, so that I might bury myself in You.* She longs to be so fully surrendered to God that she will be hidden in Him, and she knows well that her longing will be perfectly satisfied in Heaven.

The Host of Praise's existence reaches its fulfillment in Heaven where she is fully given over to the Lord and love reaches its consummation. However, she cannot be dissuaded by the long, painful wait, but rather, she must be spurred on. She recognizes that the more she is caught up in God through a faith-filled life, the more she can begin to live as in Heaven — established in God, ordered to Him, fully given to Him in love, and living according to His will — already now in this life here on earth. As her longing consumes her, she in turn is consumed as a holocaust of praise.

Through recollection and the prayer of praise, adoration, and thanksgiving, she gazes into the depths of the mystery of God and dwells with her beloved Three. She allows the Holy Spirit to wrap her in the love shared between the Father and the Son. The suffering caused by her incapacity for perfect surrender in this life becomes part of her offering as she shares in Christ's salvific suffering. Over and over again she chooses to trust and hands herself over to God's merciful love.

St. Elizabeth's health is failing. This letter to the newly ordained Fr. Chevignard is penned after six weeks' convalescence. She is about to begin her ten-day private retreat. The retreat marks the beginning of a new work God initiates in her, and ultimately it ushers her into a more complete understanding of her vocation as a praise of glory, now with a particular implication of conformity to Christ Crucified. Unknown to anyone, Elizabeth will die in just thirteen months.

Once again Elizabeth came to recognize God's will as expressed in a name. The extraordinary physical sufferings caused by Addison's disease helped her see herself more and more as a *sacrifice of praise.* At the physical level, God was consuming her as a holocaust in the terrible fire of systemic inflammation raging through her body as she drew nearer to her death. But long before the symptoms of her disease appeared, He was already consuming her in love precisely to make her His, conformed to Him as a sacrifice of praise. In the final months of her life conformity with Christ's sacrifice clearly became the key of her hymn of praise. This letter is an early intimation of that truth.

Departing On a Great Voyage

Retreats and other times for extraordinary solitude and silence are essential. Taking extra time out of our normal routine to dedicate ourselves to prayer allows for much-needed particular graces. Among these are those that lead to a greater surrender to the Holy Spirit's creative action in us. In silence's profound poverty, attachments and self-will are recognized and relinquished. The Spirit's creative action then takes on new forms and emphases. Ultimately, these illuminations of the Spirit bring about a more docile receptivity and help conform us more perfectly to God All-Love. Having prepared to enter this time of silence, Elizabeth arrives with a request of her own for the young priest:

> *I am departing this evening on a great voyage ... in these days I am going to be in even more absolute solitude, having some extra hours for prayer and going about the monastery with lowered veil. The sister of your soul will live the life of a desert hermit, but before burying herself there ... she feels a great need to ask for the assistance of your prayers, especially for one extraordinary intention at the Holy Sacrifice of the Mass. When you consecrate the host in which Jesus, "who alone is the Holy One," is incarnated, would you consecrate me with Him, "as a sacrifice of praise to His glory," so all my hopes, all my inclinations, all my actions, give glory to His Holiness.* (L 244)

Solitude, silence, and praise culminate for St. Elizabeth in the eucharistic sacrifice. As she begins her descent into deep silence and deep recollection, Elizabeth wants her praise to be truly united to Christ's own praise of the Father at its consummation in His self-oblation in the eucharistic liturgy. Elizabeth had already recognized that Christ dwelling in her necessarily implicated her in His Sacrifice. Now she asks for Fr. Chevignard's assistance in order to live her participation in Christ's self-offering most perfectly. *Consecrate me as a "sacrifice of praise."*

St. Elizabeth wants to be united entirely to Him, allowing Him to pray His prayer in her, being made holy with His holiness, so that, *clothed with God* her life becomes nothing other than a praise of Him.

Her prayer is the opening of the floodgates to a torrent of most extraordinary graces. Her simple *fiat* to being consumed calls down Heaven's blessed Fire. During the seclusion of these retreat days, she wants to understand in the depths of her soul Christ's call to holiness. Quoting 1 Peter 1:15 she explains, *"Be holy as I am Holy"; these are His words I keep in mind as I enter into recollection.*

She seeks this holiness in the Church at the liturgy. Through the hands of the priest, in the act of Consecration of the bread and wine into Jesus, the Host handed over and the Blood poured out, her offering is perfected. Elizabeth wants her hymn to accompany Jesus' own Sacrifice of Praise. At the moment of Consecration this *sacrifice of praise to His glory* will become *another humanity in which God renews His mystery,* and in this she is united with the Crucified in His eternal *Sanctus.* Elizabeth knows that the lyre of her silent soul has its most beautiful note drawn by the Holy Spirit from the string of suffering (HF 43). As this lyre plays its melody in chorus with the divine harmonies of the eucharistic liturgy, the Mass, her eternal *Sanctus* echoes ever-greater glory.

St. Paul helps Elizabeth appreciate that she will be made holy only through Jesus, *who alone is the Holy One.* She quotes Ephesians 1:4, writing, *St. Paul explains and comments on this when he says: "Throughout eternity, God has chosen us in Christ so that we may be immaculate, holy before Him in love"* (L 244).

Even in the shadows of this life, the bright promise of God's grace and His plan for our sanctification illuminate her path and her offering. There is no need for her to be worried about the purity or worthiness of her offering. The Lord asks for everything in an act of trust-filled surrender. She is a baptized believer. She knows that grace precedes and encompasses her. *Throughout eternity, God has chosen us in Christ so that we may be immaculate, holy before Him in love.*

It is His work in her, more than her work. Over and over again, Elizabeth confides her misery, her sins, and her weakness through acts of surrender to God's super-abundant mercy. She takes as her own His power, His holiness, His glory. She develops this eucharistic thought even until the final weeks of her life: *When we receive Christ with inner devotion … the likeness of His virtues comes to us, and He lives in us and we in Him. He gives His soul in that fullness of grace by which the soul perseveres in love and praise of the Father!"* (HF 18).

Simple, loving surrender to All-Love is the beginning of transformation and union with God and is too its final consummation. This surrender is learned, practiced, increased, and perfected in the common events of our lives. The mundane is, so to speak, transubstantiated, like bread into Eucharist, as we offer it in surrender to Love.

Recognizing Love's divine impact, which reaches even the abyss of her deep need, Elizabeth places herself within the trinitarian communion through the eucharistic sacrifice, and from there she offers herself. Her praise is buried within Jesus' Sacrifice offered to the Father on Calvary in the communion of the Holy Spirit. Her secret is to remain in Love. *Deus caritas est.* She wants the Father to strengthen her through His Spirit, so that *Christ might dwell through faith in her heart, rooting and grounding her in love, so that she may know the love of Christ and be filled according to the fullness of God* (see Eph. 3:17). It is precisely by surrendering herself completely and being offered as a victim of praise wholly consumed that she enters most deeply into the Trinity's own loving. Here is perfect union with All-Love. A month later, she will exhort the same young priest, *Let us listen to Him in the silence of our prayer, for He is the "Source" who speaks within us … May He make us sacrificial beings … sacrifice is simply love put into action"* (L 250).

St. Elizabeth desires that we also be made holy with God's own holiness through *love put into action,* a life filled with death-to-self and self-forgetfulness, acts of detachment and sacrifice, silence and prayer, union and love. In this way we allow God to consecrate us as sacrifices of praise to His glory, wholly consumed. Our total, trustful surrender to Love through intentional, recollected abiding in His presence, silent in our hearts before the Indwelling God, promises our total transformation. As we are drawn beyond our self into surrendered silence in the abyss of Love, He will make us holocausts of praise. We will share in the hidden splendor of triune Love. We will extend Jesus' love, glorifying God in our own sacrificial love poured out for others to the end.

A Love That Seeks Union

Even before the letter we just examined, St. Elizabeth meditated on the eucharistic dimensions of self-offering in earlier letters to her brother-in-law when he was still a seminarian. In June 1903, she starts with a verse that introduces the account of the Last Supper in the Gospel of John. *Having loved his own who were in the world, He loved them to the end* (see John 13:1). This is the love that Christ reveals that seeks union and solicits faith:

> *How can anyone say more about the love in the heart of God than the Eucharist? Union, consummation, He in us, we in Him, is this not Heaven on earth? It is Heaven in faith while awaiting the longed-for face-to-face vision. We will be content at last when His glory appears, when we see Him in His light. Do you not find that the soul rests in the thought of this encounter, this coming together with the One whom she so singularly loves? Everything else disappears at last and it seems that we already penetrate the mystery of God!* (L 165)

Silent wonder before the Eucharist, Christ crucified by love, opens new vistas of understanding about what it means to be a host of praise.

The final consummation and union of the soul with God in Heaven is made real in the Eucharist, if only through the dark veil of faith. Everything else disappears into the background before this eruption of the Mystery of the Godhead into our lives.

Elizabeth has not yet assumed Host of Praise as her personal name. Yet she does lay out a context for understanding this identity with subtle reference to St. John of the Cross's doctrine of *night,* which illuminates the eucharistic foundation of her identity. Host of Praise turns us to the eucharistic Host offered in the Holy Sacrifice of the Mass and adored in exposition. In relating her community's experience in adoration, she describes how contemplation of the eucharistic Christ allows Him to communicate His whole mystery to a soul: *The language of the Word is the bestowing of the gift.... He speaks in silence to our soul — while we possess the vision in substance under the humble Host. Yes, truly the Same He is who both the blessed contemplate in light and we adore in faith.*

Elizabeth explains that the community has been in eucharistic adoration from Ascension to Pentecost awaiting a new outpouring of the Holy Spirit. She marvels that before the humble Host exposed, her community possesses the substance of Heaven's vision. What the saints behold clearly is what her community contemplates in the shadows of faith. For St. Elizabeth, drawing from St. Paul, *Faith is a face-to-face in the shadows.*

There is a powerful association between the faith required for contemplative prayer and for the Eucharist. Every sacrament is a visible sign of the invisible grace, hidden in the sign, hidden in the shadows of what is seen. Approached with faith, the Eucharist is a hidden *face-to-face* in the most excellent way. This link of faith to the Eucharist is extended, moreover, as the offering of oneself in the sometimes-painful night of faith that is united to the sacrificial offering of the Eucharist.

Elizabeth starts with an assertion: when it comes to the heart of God, the Eucharist says it all. Her insight implies that this eucharistic self-communication enables us to give our hearts in return. It does this because it is a sacrament of faith, *mysterium fidei*. God communicates His love through this sacrament. So we return to St. Elizabeth's question: *How can anyone say more about the love in the heart of God than the Eucharist?*

The connection that she makes between the vision of the saints in glory and our vision "in the shadows" unveils the manner by which we receive God's love. We receive this eucharistic transformation only by belief in what we cannot see. We must come to adore Christ *in the shadows,* precisely where He seems absent. He is truly there, but the imagination, feelings, and understanding fail to fathom Him without the illuminating light of glory.

This kind of dark faith finds its source and summit in the Eucharist. In the Blessed Sacrament, Christ Crucified communicates eternal life under the veil. In the shadows of what appears as mere bread and wine, He gives *Himself* to us — not only when we receive Communion, but also when we simply behold Him. The substance of glory hidden by the humble *Host* transforms those who contemplate it. Host means victim, offering. Those who contemplate this Saving Victim become what their faith beholds: an acceptable offering to the Father, a participation in Christ's self-offering for our salvation, a host of praise joined to Christ in His atoning work.

In such prayer, Christ's love remains obscure. He may seem absent, as if He has abandoned the soul. The soul may feel empty and maybe even suffer from a sense of God's displeasure. Prayer can seem to be a waste of time. One gives oneself but seemingly receives nothing in return. Precisely at this moment, when making an act of love becomes a sacrifice, one approaches the imitation of the Crucified who loved *until the end,* and *this* is participation in Christ's act of redemptive love on the Cross. The soul is being transformed into a victim, a host of praise.

Here our feelings and intuition betray us. What seemed to be abandonment is in fact a divine inflow. The Lord is communicating His sacrificial love by joining us to His Sacrifice through our own act of sacrificial love. Christ's brilliant clarity illuminates the soul as a *ray of darkness* not because He is dark but because the soul has not yet learned to see. In offering up our own sense of abandonment and loneliness, *for love of Him*, the soul becomes like a fountain of His sacrificial love which it receives from Christ Crucified.

> *Pray that I might fully live out my bridal dowry, that I may be wholly available, wholly vigilant in faith so the master can bear me wherever He wishes. May I stay near Him who entirely grasps this mystery in order to learn everything from Him.* (L 165)

A devotion that is spousal in its faithfulness renders a soul docile in eucharistic contemplation. A bride holds nothing back from her beloved, and St. Elizabeth invites us to share this movement of her heart. This is possible thanks to her conformity to Christ and to His surrender to the loving will of the Father, which He shares with us in the nuptial banquet of the Eucharist. As at a wedding feast, this sacred feast fills the heart with a fullness of union and consummation. Such union and consummation are gifts to be welcomed. This welcome is in the form of a bridal surrender to the Bridegroom. In this surrender, Elizabeth's striking nuptial references imply mutual intimacy and mutual understanding, even if in the darkness.

Christ left this memorial of His passion as a pattern to be contemplated, pondered, wondered over, and imitated by love. It fulfills the heart's desire. Sacramental signs of thanksgiving, instituted the night before He died, unveil to faith what reason cannot see. In this thanksgiving to the Father, Jesus entrusts the total gift of Himself to us. And this gift is fulfilling. The eucharistic liturgy is a sacred banquet for the hungry.

Faith reaches out to the perfect fulfillment that is awaiting us when His glory appears in Heaven. Even now, simply pondering the unique manner of His love helps us find rest, peace for our souls. The Eucharist is a true foretaste of Heaven. That is, this sacrament discloses what is to come. As we turn our hearts to this mystery, we already begin to enter into the "rest" we are meant to have for all eternity.

Eucharistic contemplative prayer is oriented toward adoration, the surrender of one's life to God. This is paradoxical: to enter into silent prayer is to embrace a certain solitude even to the point of loneliness, and yet the Eucharist is, at the same time, a fulfilling encounter, a union and consummation. Union requires freedom, and freedom requires space — one must be set apart from all else in order to love *to the end*.

Spending time in silence before the Blessed Sacrament, both at Mass and in private prayer, helps us find this space in which everything can *disappear* until we are free to *penetrate* the depths of God. The disappearing and penetrating are caused by the same love that the Eucharist discloses, drawing us from our scattered concerns to the One we love. As we behold the Host offered for us and, through the sacrificial offering of faith, hand ourselves over as a host of praise, we penetrate further into the mystery of God. Then all else disappears and we enjoy a foretaste of perfect union with the Trinity. The night of faith is then seen as the night of intimacy shared by lovers. The Wedding Feast of the Lamb has begun. The eucharistic Christ, the Host offered in love, is the threshold into these riches.

In December 1905 she writes to Canon Angles:

> *One can feel the need to be sanctified, to disregard oneself for the sake of being fully given over to the Church's interests ... Poor France! I like covering her with the blood of the Just One, "who lives always to intercede and to plead for mercy." ... [I] must be mediatrix with Jesus Christ, to be for Him as if another humanity through which He might extend His life of reparation, sacrifice, praise, and adoration.* (L 256)

Carmelite, daughter of the Church, Elizabeth Host of Praise of the Trinity makes her life and being an occasion of God's work of sanctification for the world through her desire for souls to the point of self-forgetfulness. By remaining constantly united with God and receiving the power of His gaze, she allows God to raise her on the wings of her desire into conformity with Christ, so that she might share with Him in His work of redemption and love of souls.

Elizabeth desires to extend and multiply Jesus' acts and prayers that He offered during His earthly life for the salvation of souls. She wants to allow Him to perpetuate His life in her own life, to be made present in her and work through her. Having yielded to the purification of His love in her soul, and by continuing to give to God her whole being and existence, Elizabeth wills to share in His work by allowing Him to be her life, her fidelity, and her all. She claims nothing for herself except to be always more entirely His in order to be more perfectly *mediatrix* for Him in the work of redemption.

As lofty as Elizabeth's desires are, she remains attentive to reality. Her participation in Christ's work, the extra-added humanity she wants to be for Christ, means that she accepts what each day brings and allows Christ to be made present in it. Her first act of losing herself is to receive what is given as God's will for her, whether enjoying the sparkling stars in the night sky, accepting an interruption to her prayer, struggling against her physical frailty, or overcoming a difficulty in her work. Her poverty is to receive each moment with great detachment so that everything, pleasant or not, is welcomed as a divine gift.

Elizabeth's docility to God in the unfolding of her life will become truly heroic as her illness progresses and her physical sufferings increase. For the time being God is schooling her in abandonment and gracing her with a readiness to put on Christ as the old self dies, *quotidie morior,* as she called it. This struggle can feel endless; the dark clouds of discouragement threaten peace and the interior stillness of trustful surrender. We must allow ourselves to be consumed by our longing for union and love, as a *host-victim of praise.* We need to cultivate that yearning, despite the pain it often occasions, and to ask that Lord to make up what is lacking in us. In this way the soul finds itself buried in God through every thought, word, and act that animates our pursuit of union and love.

> *Plead with Him that I might lose myself in order to be buried in Him … at Mass, when you consecrate the host in which Jesus becomes incarnate, would you also consecrate your little child to* Love All-Powerful, *so that He may transform her "into a praise of glory." It is a great feeling to think that I am going to be given, offered up by you!* (L 256)

St. Elizabeth desires and is convinced that a praise of glory must live out her vocation within the Church, in a liturgical and sacramental life and in the daily duties of her vocation. Hers is an ecclesial soul, drawing grace from the liturgy and offering herself for the good of souls in the Church's mission to the world. She is convinced that only in union with the Sacrificial Victim offered at Mass will her self-offering be fully consummated. In the hands of the sacrificing priest, consecrated with the eucharistic Host to All-Powerful Love, Elizabeth finds the consummate means of transformation and fruitfulness that only her beloved Three can accomplish in her. This faithful little one will unite herself with the Lamb to be offered, given, surrendered, transformed, and made fruitful, by Love and according to the Father's will.

Elizabeth's awareness of her own misery and her incapacity to be holy compels her to cast herself upon the One who is Faithful and True. She prays His prayer in her, loves with His love, loses herself in Him. Accordingly, Elizabeth, the House of God, makes more space for the Lord as her self decreases and God becomes her all. The Praise of Glory allows God to substitute Himself for her until she becomes solely a radiance of His life. The Host of Praise surrenders all to Him as she is wholly consumed in His love.

Come into me, she prays, *as Adorer, as Reparator, as Savior* (*Oblation to the Trinity*), not just for her own transformation, but for the redemption of all. How will this extraordinary conformity of identity be effected in one so weak and imperfect? Elizabeth knows that only in being consecrated to Love, in descending into the deepest depths of the Abyss of Mercy, can she hope to be wholly transformed.

What Elizabeth desires and allows God to do in her can only take place through the Eucharist. At the altar, God comes anew to her in Holy Communion, to her, a house of God. At the altar, God's own life is poured into her, into her, a praise of His glory. And at the altar, Elizabeth's ultimate surrender is effected through the work of Christ the Eternal High Priest, who anchors her self-offering as Host of Praise in His perfect self-offering as the Saving Victim. Here, this House of God, Praise of Glory, and Host of Praise finds fulfilment in eucharistic Communion, life, and offering. At the altar, we in turn become bread for the world, bearing God's presence, likeness, and self-giving love. Here, the lofty calling of the Christian vocation consummated as in Heaven by faith, but only because triune Love comes down to us in the Bread from Heaven.

The Paschal Offering of All Christian Faithful

In a letter to her sister Guite, Elizabeth writes, *Dear little host of praise* (L 288). From her innermost heart, St. Elizabeth addresses Guite in this way to encourage her as a fellow contemplative called to the same heavenly existence that she herself knows. As her death draws near, Elizabeth sheds all but the essential. Her pen extracts from her soul that which is deepest and truest, the wisdom of God. In the extremes of her suffering, only the most significant realities are of any consequence. For Elizabeth, Guite is among those most significant realities. Elizabeth wants to lead her in the way of charity in the depths of her own being in prayer. She wants Guite to live there, in the abyss, because that is where a transforming encounter with God is waiting to take place.

In this letter, once again, Elizabeth is using the term *host of praise*; and not uncharacteristically, she implicates her sister in God's work in her own soul, even while she remains hidden away in Carmel. She closes her letter by ascribing this new name to her little nieces along with their mother. Over the next few months until her death, Elizabeth increasingly refers to herself with this name. The reality of the name unfolds in her life and encompasses her whole being. Like all her names, it began as an intuition in her soul but comes to mark and define her whole being.

Guite, first in importance among Elizabeth's spiritual children, humanly speaking is Elizabeth's other half. Elizabeth envisions her mission first of all in relation to Guite, *Let us sing our hymn to Love together day and night.* At times Guite seems to be an extension of Elizabeth's heart, as Elizabeth invites her to share her own mission, one sister living as love-inside-the-walls of Carmel and the other as love-in-the-world.

> *"The holiest is he who is most loving. Gazing upon God most of all, he most fully meets the needs of His gaze." Is this not so beautiful, little praise of glory? We share such deep accord over what our Maestro asks of us ... I have so many desires for your soul, or rather only one: that you love, were you but all love, were you moved but by love, were you but to make Love happy until He were to carve out His abyss in your soul and you were but always present to Him: "For the one who seeks and savors God in all things, nothing can prevent him from solitude among a whole multitude. He is invincible to anything changing his simple gaze. Unchanging before changing images; he passes beyond them, aiming at God."* (L 288)

Elizabeth recognizes the Lord's call as one and the same, inside Carmel and in the world. The Lord is Love. Guite shares in Love's symphony in her home life as Elizabeth shares in it in the cloister. The two sisters find Love's melody by dwelling in the depths of their souls, utterly occupied in loving and in being consumed by Love's good pleasure.

The interior solitude where Elizabeth dwells alone with the Maestro is, paradoxically, a mutual solitude, shared not only with Guite, but with all those who pursue her adored Three. Love is mysterious like that. The soul is solitary with the Holy One, yet it is within the communion of the Body of Christ. Love's claim is intimate and exclusive, but also common and universal. Perhaps it is not as strange as it seems, for *the loving heart lives no longer in itself, but in the one who is the object of its love*. Having been taken up into the very love of the Divine Persons, the soul is being transformed into God Himself and therefore shares in that great mystery of the One and the Three.

It is worth noting here the comments of a former postulant who recorded her memories from her time in the Dijon Carmel during this period. She said that Sr. Elizabeth of the Trinity was always deeply recollected — during her daily chores, at recreation, in prayer. God, it seemed, was always present to Sr. Elizabeth. However, this face-to-face abiding, Elizabeth's experience of Heaven lived by faith, did not make her unavailable to the other nuns. She was always ready, with a smile and a kind and gentle word, to give assistance as needed, but her gaze was *heavenly*. Elizabeth beheld God as she lived out the duties of her Carmelite vocation. The Host of Praise stood on the brink of Heaven living a sacrificial life of love and service on earth.

The steadiness of such a soul, consumed by love and always dwelling humbly before God's gaze, becomes a refuge for those who spend time in her company. It is refreshing to be with a contemplative soul, especially in today's world, marked as it is by a flux of changing images flashing past us so quickly that oftentimes we fail to see the images themselves and only experience the uneasiness that comes from being accosted by the noisy barrage and chaos. Especially now, we need to become oases of the powerful calm of true interior silence. We must allow God to clothe us in *the name of the Lord [which] is a strong tower*, so that our presence can be a refuge for others. From within the security of such a sanctuary, a deeper surrender to love is possible. The pursuit of Love above all else can then be shared and become superabundantly fruitful in the Church and in the whole world. What does this pursuit of love require?

> *Chanting together our hymn of love, both day and night, "I want to awaken the dawn." I mean to say that before dawn appears, I love already!... To love is so simple. It means to be given over to all His intentions in the same way that He surrendered to those of the Father. It means to abide in Him. For this reason, the heart that loves no longer lives in itself, but in the one who is the object of its love. This means to suffer for Him. It means gathering together with joy each and every sacrifice, each and every self-offering that allow us to give joy*

> *to His Heart. May He Himself teach you the art of love in your interior solitude. I gaze upon you in mine. I sense that you are quite close to me, "within me," in my heaven. It is from there that I write you.* (L 280)

For St. Elizabeth, love is simple: to surrender, to dwell in, to suffer for Him. Love's absolute simplicity undergirds all of the spiritual life for Elizabeth. She abides in loving, in all her comings and goings, with her whole being. It is always the time for loving. Her refuge is to remain buried in God as House of God; she returns herself as a gift to Him for the praise of His glory; and she surrenders to being consumed for Love's sake as Host of Praise.

Elizabeth instructs Guite, and us, about the asceticism of love. The virtue of charity overcomes the old self for the praise of Love Himself. It takes up the cross through simple sacrifices and joyfully offered sufferings. It bears life's annoyances with patience and lightheartedness, overlooking slights and insults and finding small words and gestures of kindness that may otherwise remain unnoticed. This participation in Christ's supreme act of reparation is often hidden in the outwardly insignificant moments of the day; but if they are hidden in love, they are endowed with salvific power.

The indwelling Trinity that Elizabeth has perceived since her early childhood was a Fire of Love, burning in her deepest recesses and refining her. This Heaven of the Trinity is a haven that is at the same time a furnace. The ravaging power of the divine love of the *God who is a consuming fire* prepares the soul to give itself over to loving, as self-preoccupation is burned up in it. With the soul's self-centeredness consumed, there is more space for the other, and therefore greater possibility for deeper communion.

It is as if Elizabeth intends for God to instruct Guite in the art of love within the embrace of Elizabeth's own relationship with Him.

Surely it is so. This is just how the Mystical Body functions: "So we, though many, are one body in Christ, and individually members one of another" (Rom. 12:5). The communion into which God draws us when we gaze on Him gazing at us is the context within which He will love others through us. The Fire of Love that consumes as it spreads, also warms and unites in Love. This was Elizabeth's desire for Guite, and in the divine union with her Beloved she desires to establish an invincible place for her sister and for us under God's gaze of love — a gaze from those eyes burning like a flame of fire and drawing us into the love that consumes and unites:

I ASK MY THREE FOR A BLESSING FOR MY ... DEAR LITTLE HOLOCAUSTS OF PRAISE

In October 1906, Elizabeth writes to Germaine de Gemeaux:

> *Oh, you cannot imagine how divine the days pass for your friend in Carmel! A little weaker from day to day, I sense that the Maestro will delay no more in coming to find me. I taste, I experience unfamiliar joys. The joy of suffering, oh! beloved Germaine, how gentle and sweet it is!... Before dying, I dream of being transformed into Jesus Crucified. This dream gives me such strength in suffering... Beloved sister, we must not have any other ideal than to be conformed to this Divine Model. With what ardor would we bear our sacrifice, with what contempt of ourselves, if we but kept the eyes of the heart turned toward Him.* (L 324)

We find the almost paradoxical situation of the Host of Praise, consumed by suffering yet also consumed with the joy of love as she reaches toward Heaven. A few weeks before her death, St. Elizabeth speaks of divinely passing days, not in the midst of bliss, but in agony. It is a curious progression of thought: *How divine the days pass ... a little weaker from day to day . . . I taste, I experience unfamiliar joys. The joy of suffering . . . how gentle and sweet it is!* What is it that empowers Elizabeth to find Heaven in the midst of her pain? Her answer is, *I dream of being transformed into Jesus Crucified. This dream gives me such strength in suffering.*

Elizabeth's practice of interior recollection affects not just her set times of mental prayer but her whole life. She wants to be like Jesus, to be more intimately united with Him, and since this requires suffering, she is eager to embrace it. It is not suffering for its own sake that brings her joy, but her suffering as part of God's plan for eternal glory in Christ. She continues her letter with this thought: *If you knew the unspeakable joy that my soul tastes when I ponder how the Father has predestined me to be conformed to His crucified Son. . . . St. Paul shares with us the divine election that seems to be my share!*

Her eyes are fixed on Christ, but the whole Christ in His eternal mystery. This includes Jesus on the Cross, whose prayer is *eternally living and present before the Father* as she says, but also Jesus seated at the right hand of the Father in His eternal glory, where *our life is hidden with Christ in God.* Eternity or the *Standing Now* (*Nunc Stans,* for Aquinas, *Summa Theologica* I, q. 10, art. 2, ad 1) gathers up into the eternal present all of time. As Elizabeth says elsewhere, the present moment is *eternity begun, but still in progress* (LR 1). Likewise, eternity gives us access to both the Cross of Christ from the past and the future glory held out to us in the glorified Christ. It is in this eternity that Elizabeth strives to dwell, and this eternal perspective transfigures daily life, even suffering.

Although Elizabeth does not quote from Colossians 3:1–4 in this letter, its key ideas are pervasive here and throughout her thought — especially the call to set our hearts on things above, not on earthly things, for *we died* — united with Jesus on the Cross — *and our life is hidden with Christ in God* — grasped now through faith and hope. Elizabeth's spirituality and interior prayer emphasize eternity. She strives to live in the realm of eternity. She keeps in mind an eternal perspective as she goes through her days, and this transfigures these days into something divine, heavenly, even while they are filled with the most ordinary tasks and with intense suffering. Elizabeth gently explains, *Beloved sister of my soul, in the light of eternity God makes me understand so many things. I am telling you as if on His behalf: do not to be afraid of sacrifice, of struggle, but instead savor it all the more.* Days of suffering can be considered *heavenly days* only in light of eternity and the fruit that such struggles can bear into eternity.

Elizabeth wants to live anchored in Heaven's realities while still on earth, by faith and hope. Faith and hope do actually attain to those realities, even if as through a veil. This is why there can be such quiet in contemplation: because we are beginning to rest in our final end, God Himself. Even as careful a thinker as Aquinas insists that faith terminates not in propositions or articles of faith but in the reality itself (*res*), the reality of God (ST II-II, q. 1, art. 2, ad 2). Elizabeth is on solid theological ground when she reaches out in faith and hope to live the life of Heaven even on earth, in communion with the triune God dwelling in her soul.

We are meant to dwell on the threshold of eternity stretching out toward it. For example, when we begin a prayer, whether an Our Father or the Jesus Prayer, we might hope to break through into eternity, that stretching out toward the Lord, we may break through into His eternal embrace. All is very calm and peaceful there on the brink of eternity. And if we are sleepy in prayer, it is a good way to rouse ourselves a little. Just a little while and we will see the Lord face-to-face, heart-to-heart. Heaven is just a blink away. Even now in faith, however, He is already present regardless of fatigue or mood or even severe suffering. It is a simple decision to believe, a simple surrender of faith. With this next prayer, with this next act of love, my faith breaks into eternity. Prayer offered with this faith keeps us rooted in the truth that life passes and the next life quickly comes, but the substance of what is to come is already present even in suffering. This helps us anchor our own outlook in God's eternal perspective.

Another way that Elizabeth's days of suffering are *divine*: they are days in which she grows *weaker from day to day*. In our weakness, His strength reaches perfection. She expands upon this theme as she encourages Germaine not to give in to discouragement in her weakness but to trust in God, utterly dependent upon Him: *Do not be discouraged, do not become sad. I would submit to you: love your misery for in it God exercises His mercy ... The more you feel your weakness, the more your confidence must grow, for on Him alone you must rely* (L 324).

Utter dependence on God in this life prefigures the life of Heaven. In Heaven, God's life will be our very life to the full, in glorious splendor, sharing in the Divine Nature. As the supernatural life increases in us, so too does our dependence on God. We need not fear our weakness but should rejoice in the dependence on God that it implies. We cannot be too needy or desperate for God; He will fill our emptiness to overflowing. "Blessed are the poor in spirit, for theirs is the kingdom of heaven" (Matt. 5:3). Elizabeth already has a taste of Heaven precisely in her poverty of spirit and utter dependence on God. Amidst her suffering as a host of praise, she already possesses something of the joy of the blessed. With the light of eternity shining in our souls, we also can come to taste the blessedness of dependence on God, who one day soon will be *all in all.*

Surrender and Trusting Self-Abandonment

At the end of June 1906, Elizabeth sends a letter to her young friend, Louise Demoulin.

> *I ask the Lord to be Himself your Maestro, your Friend, your Confidant, your Strength. May He make of your soul a little heaven where He can rest with happiness. Cut out anything in it that could wound His divine gaze. He loves brave and generous hearts. Recall that love must culminate in sacrifice. When he speaks of the Maestro, Saint Paul says: "He loved me, He gave Himself up for me" (Gal 2:20). May His holy will be the double-edged sword that ceaselessly immolates you. To learn this art, draw close to Jesus in the agony of the garden as His crushed soul cries out: "Thy will be done. not mine."* (L 291)

Desire and surrender is a basic rhythm in life, a pattern that everyone experiences. It takes many shapes and forms and concerns the gravest to the most trivial matters. Caught up in a particular circumstance, we might not notice we are once again in the cycle of desire and surrender; yet, pondering the events of life over time, this basic pattern is easily discerned. This is the heartbeat of a host of praise. You pour yourself out into a project or mission, dedicating months or years, only to have to surrender the project because of circumstances beyond your control. Parents devote themselves to raising their child and the Lord calls the child to Himself in an early death. For years a religious devotes himself to formation in a community, but in the end he is not accepted for solemn profession. After months of intense prayer, an undesired resolution is granted. Lord, what happened? Why another sacrifice?

St. Elizabeth shares how Our Lord Jesus too entered into this cycle of desire and surrender. "Abba, Father, all things are possible to thee; remove this cup from me; yet not what I will, but what thou wilt" (Mark 14:36). Jesus expressed His desire to His Heavenly Father with cries and pleading, yet He remained surrendered to the will of the Father.

A false response to this cycle of desire and surrender is to say, "If the surrender of my desires may be required of me, it is better not to desire." In an attempt to protect ourselves from hurt and pain, we might choose not to accept the risk of love and desire. Ironically, trying to protect ourselves from suffering ends miserably. By allowing no one else in, we are left alone, even while externally we may be engaged with all types of social circles. Offering our self as a host or holocaust of praise moves in the opposite direction and leads to freedom and the discovery of our true self, precisely by losing oneself in surrender. God's offer of love and communion remains amidst all human loss. So Elizabeth directs Louise to Him, *I ask the Lord to be Himself your Maestro, your Friend, your Confidant, your Strength* (L 324).

God died for love of our love, out of His desire to be loved by us. He wants us to have a strong desire for Him and for all created things that lead to Him. There cannot be too great a desire in the spiritual life, because there cannot be too much love. Desire needs to be ordered rightly and at times go beyond sensible desire into a gentle burning in the spirit as the will is drawn up into the Lord in charity. But desire must always increase because love should be growing. Elizabeth points out, *He loves brave and generous hearts.* Times of ardent desire may give way to times of surrender that purify and deepen our desire. God may ask for a shift in our desire, from the good of created things, or from the good of consolations, more to Himself.

The rhythm of desire and surrender seems to pervade all of creation. In exercising charity our spiritual heart may grow stronger in loving precisely through this cycle of desire and surrender ordained by God. From desire, to surrender, to greater desire, to surrender, to desiring higher things, to surrender, to complete correspondence with the Lord and His ways, ardently desiring what and only what the Lord does — such seems to be love's progression.

Put more delicately, to come to have a *full heart* means to have a full range of the joys and sufferings of life. God's wise plan arranges these things according to what is best for us, and the cycle of desire and surrender allows us to enter into the process of attaining a heart that loves fully. A human heart fully alive with love is offered as a pleasing host of praise to the Lord of Love.

The Lord wants our strong desire, but a desire led by *Another*. Strong desire can become stubborn or obstinate; we can become stuck in our own ways. A strong will can become self-willed. Elizabeth's pastor observed her strong will as a child and commented that because of it, she would become either a saint or a devil. A tenacious will and steadfast desire can do much to help build the kingdom of God and can help us ascend the mountain of God, but surrender needs to meet the twists and turns of God's plan, so that the soul is not self-willed but God-willed. God desires our strong desire, surrendered to Him. These cycles of desire and surrender can bring us into greater harmony with the Lord like a mysterious lyre attuned to Him. This requires sacrifice and a battle against self, a challenge that Elizabeth does not sugarcoat: *May His holy will be the double-edged sword that immolates you constantly.... Draw close to Jesus in the agony of the garden as His crushed soul cries out: "Thy will be done not mine."*

In her *Oblation to the Trinity*, Elizabeth surrenders herself to the Lord as His prey. She desires to be snatched up by Him, the *Divine Eagle* (L 269). This also implies being immolated by the two-edged sword of God's holy will. This image can be helpful when we experience the pain of having our own will contradicted and immolated by the two-edged sword of God's holy will. That can feel simply like a sword piercing us! But it is a sword that slays to give life. It is the same two-edged sword mentioned in Hebrews 4:12 and it comes with all the wisdom of the Word of God, *living and active* in our life. It is unto our salvation and our greatest good and well-being as Elizabeth is quick to point out: *My little Louise, wherever you are, whatever you do, live with Him. He never leaves you, so abide with Him without ceasing. Enter into your soul's interior. You will always find Him there, desiring to make you thrive.*

Intent on our well-being, the Lord is working His plan to bring us into the depths of union with Him. In certain areas of our life, we may resist this surrender to God's holy will because it pierces like a sword. There are other areas where we may lack desire. The cycles of desire and surrender are meant to transform us in preparation for a most intimate and eternal union with God. They make us a living host of praise, a living sacrifice offered to God with vibrant love, a self-giving that is glimpsed even now in contemplative prayer. In her *Oblation to the Trinity*, Elizabeth highlights the surrender and receptivity to God's action that is required. In prayer she asks, *May I be entirely present to you, taken up in my faith, wholly adoring, completely* surrendered *to your creative Action.*

Contemplative union is about love — love as desire, as surrender, as harmonious union. The deeper modes of prayer call us to be more receptive to the Lord's action while we give our wholehearted *Yes!* We follow the Lord's lead and second His action in our souls with a fullness of desire — even as our desire becomes more subtle and imperceptible.

The correspondence of the soul to God in contemplative prayer, being led as in a gentle dance of love, is achieved in part through the lifelong process of desire, surrender, and desire made stronger, purer, and more docile. This desire-surrender rhythm enters our life as God draws us deeper into contemplative prayer and the union of love. The Lord is making us more receptive and responsive to His action within our soul. Everything is meant to bring us into more intimate union with the Lord, so as Elizabeth has advised, *Wherever you are, whatever you do, live with Him. He never leaves you, so abide with Him without ceasing. Enter into your soul's interior. You will always find Him there, desiring to make you thrive.* This is the case, even as the Host of Praise is being wholly consumed.

To her mother:

> *It is the good God who is pleased to immolate His little host, but this Mass that He says with me, in which His love is the priest, may still last a long time. This little victim, remaining in the Hands of Him who sacrifices her, does not find the time excessive and she can say that even as she journeys along the way of suffering, she continues to remain on the path of true happiness, dear mother, away from which no one can take her.* (L 309)

Elizabeth is being plunged into the abyss, immolated at the hands of God All-Love, her priest. Her poverty, like that of the eucharistic Host, raised in offering to the Father, draws her into the trinitarian communion of love and there draws her into God's thirst for souls, freeing her for an exultant surrender. She is a host of praise to God's glory!

Wholly present, wholly transparent, wholly surrendered, silent, all-sacrificing, gazing adoringly upon the Father, all love and receptivity to Love, offered and consumed for others — she is Sr. Elizabeth of the Trinity, Host of Praise to God's glory. She establishes herself as an offering to be made at Mass so that in her God's love shines out, likening her countenance to His. She allows Him to sacrifice her so that she might become a fount of His Mercy in the world and so that His light might shine upon us.

Elizabeth lives now as a praise of glory to the extent that she is *host*. God All-Love, the great High Priest, holds her in His hands as a bride of the divine Bridegroom.

> *The Maestro deigned to choose your daughter, the fruit of your womb, to associate her with the great work of redemption. He suffers in her like an extension of His passion… The bride is the Bridegroom's; mine has taken me. He wants me to be a super-added humanity in which He can continue to suffer for the glory of His Father, to help the needs of His Church.* (L 309)

Her interior union with the Bridegroom to make up what is lacking in His sufferings, her self-offering as a host of praise in conformity with Christ, her surrender and joyful acceptance of the Father's will in all circumstances — all these lofty movements and inclinations of her soul must be lived out concretely. She shares her *secret* with her mother, encouraging her to draw near to the beloved Three.

> *All is in the intention; we can sanctify the little things, transform the most mundane deeds in divine acts! A soul that lives in union with God does nothing other than the supernatural, then the most ordinary actions, rather than separating her from Him, ensure that more and more everyday they are united.* (L 309)

This is lived faith expressed in charity, Heaven on earth through faith. Elizabeth has become Christ's super-added humanity. By remaining in prayer before God, abiding with Him, all that she does is united to the divine activity of the Blessed Trinity. Her understanding of holiness as *union and love* (L 191) once again reveals itself. Elizabeth's continual appeals for others to join her in this apostolic life in the

Trinity underscore how intensely she herself longs for her abiding to be made a fruitful participation in Christ's redemptive act.

Elizabeth knows, and here encourages her mother, that in God's providence we can contribute, so to speak, to Christ's salvific act by allowing Him to animate our thoughts, words, and acts. By prayerfully uniting ourselves with patience and gratitude in obedience to the Father's will, our death-to-self becomes an expression of our love for God. God's love begets our love, by which He draws us closer to Himself. We are conformed to Christ and enter more deeply into His interior prayer. This gives rise to further conformity and greater love. As Elizabeth approaches death, her consecration as a host of praise shares in the consummation of Christ's eucharistic Consecration. Both appear to be made of common elements of this life, whether bread or little deeds, but both are fully handed over and full of love.

Every irritation and sacrifice come to be experienced as true joy. Elizabeth explains this a few weeks later to her mother in another letter. She describes this type of joy as the *joy of the will* and she distinguishes it from the kind of joy one experiences from sensory pleasure. *Try to put joy ... into every irritation, every sacrifice.* This prepares for the emptiness and death-to-self that need to be experienced in order to be fully conformed to Christ. That holy joy indicates our docile receptivity of everything and everyone that God allows throughout the day. Elizabeth promises a satisfying peace in the soul's recesses and conformity to Him as the fruits of this willed joy.

At the time of this letter to her mother, Elizabeth has completed writing *Heaven in Faith,* the retreat she composed for her sister, as well as the retreat notes of *Last Retreat,* written for her Carmelite sisters. Her understanding of her vocation as Praise of Glory and Host of Praise continues to be refined through her oblation of suffering and the surrender of her will to God's. Her physical suffering is extreme. She has only weeks remaining until the final surrender of death is consummated. She loves to the end. During this period, she asks of her mother: *At the Elevation of the Holy Mass, place yourself with the Virgin at the foot of the Cross to offer your children together to the Heavenly Father, "whose entire will is one of love"* (L 308).

CONCLUSION

The Gift and Task of Becoming Who God Created Us to Be

The book of Revelation promises *a new name* to those who are victorious and attain the gift of Heaven. This name contains the mystery of who we are. It is how God will see us for all eternity. If grace is the seed of glory, then even now this new name belongs to us and stamps our deepest self as a new creation in Jesus Christ. It can begin as a simple, seed-like intuition, yet it comes to define our whole existence, our life's mission, and our very identity. God already begins to speak that name to us here in this life, and it echoes out from our being, shaping all our relationships and actions. Become who you are!

St. Elizabeth's names — House of God, Praise of Glory, and Host of Praise — provided her some insight into the mysterious new name she would come to enjoy for eternity in Heaven. She captured a glimpse of her deepest identity in Christ already in this life, and this helped her to grow into this identity. In the indwelling Trinity she already enjoyed *Heaven in faith* in this life, and in His call and by grace, she enjoyed a foretaste of her new heavenly name and the particular intimacy of God's eternal love for her. This life of faith and hope shaped her and her actions as she stretched forward toward the life of Heaven. She became the saint that God destined her to be by fixing her eyes on All-Love dwelling within.

So too for us, laying hold of our deepest identity in Christ through faith and hope helps us to live out this identity in charity already in this life. In fixing our hearts and minds on things above, we do not leave our earthly life and relationships behind; we allow God to transfigure them according to His perfect will. Fixing our eyes on high helps us to receive things from on high. This in turn elevates us in accord with God's designs for us.

By receiving a name like House of God with interior conviction, we can begin to think of ourselves in these terms. I am not simply what I do, or the roles I fulfill, or my appearance. My value is not determined by the world's standards. As House of God, what is most fundamental about me is that *I am* a dwelling place of God. My beloved Three is more intimate to me than I am to myself. Ultimately, this is what is most deeply true of me.

Being a praise of glory, it becomes connatural for me to put God's glory before my own desires or self-seeking. Thinking of myself in this way, as who I am, helps me to spontaneously radiate God's love to others. I allow myself to be loved and to step out boldly in faith in accord with this love and high calling in Christ. As a praise of glory, I allow the Holy Spirit to do His work and play me as a harp, making of my life a canticle of praise to God. The duties and minutiae of my life then are no longer drab and dreary but a beautiful song of praise to God.

By living with faith as Host of Praise, I identify myself according to my relationship with the One who receives my offering. After thought, action follows. Events and situations in life no longer seem random, simply making life difficult and seemingly meaningless. Rather, I receive these things as forming me into the Host of Praise I am, and I respond with my sacrifice of love. Mass after Mass together make up the links of the chain of my life, as I live out the Eucharist and am taken up as the Host of Praise. It is who I have become.

How will you see life and your very self? As God sees them or as the world sees them? To grow into the truth of yourself as House of God, Praise of Glory, and Host of Praise, let it be done unto you according to your faith!

PART III

Oblation to the Trinity—Captivated, Caught Up, Consumed

INTRODUCTION

THE THREE NAMES IN ELIZABETH'S *OBLATION TO THE TRINITY*

NOW WE COME TO the crowning gem of St. Elizabeth's legacy to us, her *Oblation to the Trinity*. We refer to it as a prayer of oblation because of how much is drawn from St. Thérèse of Lisieux's *Oblation to Merciful Love*. What St. Thérèse expresses through the Old Testament language of "oblation of holocaust," St. Elizabeth unveils in Mary's "surrender" in the New Testament's Annunciation. What St. Elizabeth writes is in the same genre of self-offering. Of course, she herself did not entitle the prayer in this way. Traditionally the words with which she begins this prayer, *O My God Trinity whom I Adore,* have been used instead of a title. In this meditation on the names of St. Elizabeth, we wish to emphasize the oblationary surrender that she makes of herself to the Trinity as *prey* and her desire to *bury* or entomb herself in the Trinity. On this basis, we and others refer to this work as the *Oblation* or *Oblation to the Trinity*.

> *O My God, Trinity whom I adore, help me to forget myself entirely in order to be established in You, still and peaceful, as if my soul were already in eternity. May nothing trouble my peace, nor make me leave You, O my Immutable. But may each moment carry me into the depths of Your Mystery. Calm my soul; make it Your heaven, Your beloved dwelling and Your resting place. May I never forsake You there, but instead may I be fully*

present, fully awakened in my faith, fully adoring, fully receptive to Your creative action.

O my beloved Christ, crucified by love, I desire to be a bride for Your heart, I desire to cover You with glory, I want to love You ... unto death! But I feel my weakness and I ask You to "clothe me with Yourself." Identify my soul with all the movements of Your soul. Overwhelm me, invade me, substitute Yourself for me, until my life is nothing but a radiance of Your Life. Come into me as Adorer, as Reparator, and as Savior.

O eternal Word, word of my God, I yearn to spend my life listening to You. I want to become totally docile so that I learn everything from You. Then, through all nights, all voids, all weaknesses, I want always to gaze on You and to abide in Your great light. O my beloved Star, captivate me so that I cannot leave Your splendor.

O consuming Fire, Spirit of Love, spread in me until my soul is filled, like another incarnation of the Word, that I may be for Him another humanity in whom He renews His whole Mystery.

And You, O Father, bend down over Your poor little creature, see in her only the Beloved in whom You have placed Your delight.

O my Three, my All, my Beatitude, infinite Solitude, Immensity in whom I lose myself, I surrender myself to You as Your prey. Bury Yourself in me so that I may bury myself in You, while waiting to contemplate in Your light the abyss of Your grandeurs. Amen.

Three names stamp Elizabeth's soul and shape her spirituality for this oblation: House of God, Praise of Glory, and Host of Praise. We have examined these three names in light of the Blessed Virgin Mary, *the great Praise of Glory,* and have found in her both a model and invitation to each of us to accept the mystery of who we are before God. These names also contain and reveal a new kind of freedom, the exercise of which confirms this mystery. This is to say, a name expresses both the gift and the task of becoming the person God created us to be. The gift is the truth about our being. The task is how we freely choose to live this truth or reject it. It is possible to fall short of this truth and never fully rise to the task of being who God has summoned us into existence to be. Such a failure would amount to a catastrophic self-contraction, the use of our freedom against ourselves. This is why St. Paul calls this use of freedom slavery to sin. By grace, however, a new kind of freedom is possible. This is the freedom to rise to the task of who we really are in the eyes of God. This freedom is given to us by grace that Christ won for us. If we are said to be living up to our Christian name, it means someone has recognized the graced inner freedom that our name demands for us to be as we should be before God. If her names are about newness of being, we can see Elizabeth's prayer of oblation to the Trinity as the new freedom of action that follows upon such being. If, as the ancient philosophers would say, act follows being, then St. Elizabeth drawing from the words of St. Paul witnesses to a way of being as new as the freedom that expresses it, "I have been crucified with Christ; it is no longer I who live, but Christ who lives in me; and the life I now live in the flesh I live by faith in the Son of God, who loved me and gave himself for me" (Gal. 2:20).

What do the House of God, Praise of Glory, and Host of Praise do? Elizabeth offers herself in an act of total surrender and oblation to the Blessed Trinity, becoming perfectly each, House of God,

Praise of Glory, and Host of Praise. As we consider the *Oblation* that she composed, it is not enough merely to explain this relation with hagiographic facts. A specific dynamic is at stake. A pathway for action, a personal and pastoral horizon for souls who want to enter into and live out the names of St. Elizabeth of the Trinity as dynamic realities of holiness, needs to be delineated. Here St. Elizabeth's names will be considered in relationship to her *Oblation.*

To begin, we explore how the saint as House of God is blessed to have the triune God dwelling within her soul, *interior intimo meo* (closer to me than I am to myself). With the Lord dwelling so intimately, she asks to be captivated by Him. In this way she will abide with her beloved Guest: *Calm my soul; make it Your heaven, Your beloved dwelling and Your resting place. May I never forsake You there, but instead may I be fully present, fully awakened in my faith, fully adoring, fully receptive to Your creative action.*

She knows she needs to be captivated by Him to be wholly present to Him. Elizabeth knows human tendency to become dissipated and stray from the One Thing Necessary, our north star, so to speak. *O my beloved Star, captivate me so that I cannot leave Your splendor.*

She prays to be fascinated by the Lord's beauty. Only then will she remain truly attentive and devoted to the One dwelling *at home* in her soul, captivated by His beauty and in contemplation of Him. Elizabeth is also Praise of Glory. In her *Oblation to the Trinity,* she wants to live no longer for herself but entirely for her beloved Bridegroom, covering Him in glory: *O my beloved Christ, crucified by love, I desire to be a bride for Your heart, I desire to cover You with glory, I want to love You ... unto death!*

This bridal mysticism echoes some words of St. Paul that find their true fulfillment in Christ's nuptial relationship with His Bride the Church: "The wife is the glory of her husband" (see 1 Cor. 11:7). As a bride of Christ, Elizabeth is the glory of Christ. She is a praise of glory in this spousal living-for-the-other and no longer for herself. There is a truly radical orientation to the divine Other that is implied by being a praise of glory, existing only for the Other and radiating forth His glory. Elizabeth entreats the Lord: *Overwhelm me, invade me, substitute Yourself for me, until my life is nothing but a radiance of Your Life.*

The second reflection explores this existing for the divine Other as a praise of glory, as Elizabeth expresses it in her *Oblation to the Trinity,* where she so desires to be taken up with the Other in whom she indeed is *caught up*. We must consider being enraptured by the Trinity, which as part of any act of oblation, may not be quite what one first imagines enrapturement to be. To be enrapt in the dynamic Love of the Trinity is precisely to be caught up in the movement of self-emptying love. Elizabeth as Host of Praise is she who is consumed. The last lines of her *Oblation* capture this vividly: *O my Three, my All, my Beatitude, infinite Solitude, Immensity in whom I lose myself, I surrender myself to You as Your prey. Bury Yourself in me so that I may bury myself in You, while waiting to contemplate in Your light the abyss of Your grandeurs.*

In her *Oblation* to her Three and her All, Elizabeth surrenders herself as prey, to be consumed by God—burying herself in the depths of the communion of Father, Son, and Holy Spirit, buried in Love. In seeking ever greater union with the Lord, Elizabeth is consumed by thirst. Her thirsting desire for God consumes her to the extent that she becomes an oblation. She is a whole-burnt offering and victim offered unto God and His glory as Host of Praise wholly consumed.

Finally, we consider the all-consuming thirst of the Host of Praise. Elizabeth's increasing thirst keeps driving her on toward the Lord to the point of being consumed, as she offers herself on the altar. Yet, no matter how powerful her thirsting desire was, the main impetus was actually God's thirst for Elizabeth (L 179, L 210). Whatever may be said of the God of the philosophers, on the Cross the God of Love declared His thirst for souls (CCC 2560). Elizabeth's thirst is a share in His thirst. And He is the One who sends down the *consuming Fire, Spirit of Love* upon His little Host of Praise, *burying Himself in her that she might bury herself in Him,* now being wholly consumed.

CHAPTER ONE

Captivated—The Trinity, Beauty, and Contemplation

Oh my God, Trinity whom I adore ... O my Three, my All, my Beatitude, infinite Solitude, Immensity in whom I lose myself.

St. Elizabeth of the Trinity's *Oblation to the Trinity* is the offering of a soul captivated and ravished by the beauty of God. True beauty is terrifying to behold, to contemplate; true beauty renders one vulnerable. It implies suffering the loss of self. It is not only to risk death; it is to plunge into it. Once the beauty of even a creature is perceived, everything one once lived for comes to be questioned. This was true of Adam when he beheld Eve, and even truer of Moses when he beheld God. It led Adam to hide in Paradise and filled God's Chosen People with fear at having the Lord encamp with them in the desert. If a creature can shake us to our depths, what happens when the splendor of the Lord shines upon us?

A Dramatic Contemplation

St. Elizabeth's contemplation is truly dramatic. The hero of her prayer is God, and the foe is her *self* with its pride, obsessions, rebellion, and clamoring. Without God, all the noble desires of her prayer are insufficient. With Him, a love is shared that is more powerful than death. This possessed and possessing love looks out on the sheer splendor of the terrifying beauty of God. If God is the protagonist in Christian contemplation, how can St. Elizabeth's *Oblation to the Trinity* assist us to enter into this salvific drama? The *Oblation* itself is the fruit of her prayer, her practice of silence and solitude — in which method was completely subordinate to the object of her faith, He who gave Himself up for her sake. She only has eyes for Him.

After a period of intense interior trials as a novice, St. Elizabeth's prayer became a more simplified, loving movement toward God. This was a movement of faith, a *beholding* overshadowed by an attentive paternal power that her intellect could not see, and an *attending to* an educating silence that lay beyond the grasp of her human understanding. Hers was not an empty silence, nor was her darkness confused. Rather, a Divine inflow flooded her soul, drawing her out of self and into deeper vulnerability. Not only was her mind captivated, her whole being was captivated as she was willingly made Love's prey.

In her contemplation of the Trinity, Christ's beauty beckoned, indicating the pathway for the disappearance of her "self." Total liberation from the trap of ego was necessary. The drama of her prayer began as St. John of the Cross's Dark Night once began, with the sheer good fortune of having been offered a way out. Only the soul that is forgetful of self can give itself freely in love.

God's beauty elicits her desire to be bride, to give herself entirely, even unto death. As a consequence of this noble desire, Elizabeth's prayer uncovers thoughts of inadequacy, voids, weaknesses — all tendencies to betray and contradict these magnificent movements discovered through her gaze of faith on Him. We find in her aspirations a desire to return a faithful, indissoluble love, and she confronts the tendency to unfaithfulness that threatens every excellent love. She refuses to allow her awareness of her own inadequacy to have the last word before the Great Mystery of Love. Indeed, it is always only a demonic, apparent beauty that discloses itself in order to elicit despair. Divine beauty is gracious and tender in its intentions toward us. It does not seek simply to be adored but to make the beloved who adores more beautiful and to finally be truly alive, transformed.

The enthusiasm of her invocations to the Trinity evidences the joy that this kind of prayer produces. Her heroic aspirations and declarations speak to her maturing love. Most of all, her pleas for divine help unveil an ardent humility in which both her joy and love are rooted.

Prayer Infused with Truth Incarnate

If the wholly loving movement of her prayer is joyful and humble, why would we deduce that her contemplation beholds a terrifying mystery? Along with being captivated, is there not holy awe? How can anyone sustain the courage to be so vulnerable to such great beauty for any length of time? Whoever sees the face of God, whoever beholds His splendor, has seen the Beauty for which this life is too small. Yet, God does not wish for us to forsake this life but rather to engage it with a new fervor.

This kind of prayer is able to *feel weakness* and pass through all kinds of *nights* and *voids*, gazing on and abiding in Christ's captivating brilliance. The love of Christ has seized Elizabeth's whole soul so that no matter what happens, she knows she is beloved. She wants to behold this Light, and she wants the Father to behold His own radiant beauty in her. Her prayer surrenders into Light's movements through all life's happenings.

This prayer discloses the hope that souls can have in the face of what appears to be insurmountable evil. There is an answer to this evil sown into our humanity. J. R. R. Tolkien coined the term *eucatastrophe* to identify that surprising but longed-for happy ending. It's surprising because it happens always when it seems most unlikely. It is longed for because even when it seems utterly impossible, as long as the thought of it lives in our hearts, we are enabled to face whatever might come. We can apply this idea of hope to what God is doing when our prayer seeks that radiant beauty to be free of self and established in His peace. Such prayer confronts both catastrophe — the self in all its voids, weaknesses, and nights — and at the same time eucatastrophe — that coming and present immensity in which the self is lost. This prayer faces the crisis that unveils painful truths and that longs for that ostensibly impossible happy ending knit into our very being. In all kinds of humiliations our own willfulness dies, so that a new freedom to will with love what God lovingly wills might be forged.

This freedom to love is found not in the limited efforts of our own weaknesses, but rather in the surrendering of these into His initiative; not in the product of human accomplishment, but in His own activity, power, and purpose that communicate praise and power to make reparation into the soul. It is a freedom that is not found in the absorption of the human will into the Divine, but in the weaknesses of human will, where God has freely chosen to unleash the new power, that our tired humanity was created to know and desperately needs if it is ever to rise above the futility of sin and death. Together, faithfulness, perseverance, humility, and readiness to repent and begin again give the Trinity the spaciousness needed to realize this divine work in the human heart. In the surrender of our inadequacy, through our faithfulness, and by accepting the resultant sorrows, Christ's new rule of adoration, reparation, and salvation animates our existence. This new identity unfolds to the point that we live no longer our own life, but Christ lives in us.

The contemplation of St. Elizabeth culminates in a kind of incarnation. It is subtle and hidden like the great Incarnation of the Word in the virgin womb. Her contemplation conceives anew the whole saving mystery and communicates it into the exigencies of her own existence, advancing everything to her self-offering *crucified by Love.* She is captivated and freely made captive in her whole being. As House of God, her whole being is offered to God as His dwelling-place in a kind of incarnation that deepens more and more. She becomes increasingly a dwelling that is fit for God and a place in which He is truly at home.

In this prayer of oblation, the power to bear away sin is given to animate those parts of our humanity otherwise inclined to sin. A simple act of faith, filled with love of Him, suddenly transforms a humiliation into a source of living water for the world. Beauty and terror, death and the beloved coincide in a new life of surrender — the bride's activity in and receptivity to the Bridegroom who initiates love in her weakness and vulnerability.

The Sacred Beauty of Her *Oblation*

As her prayer comes to a close, the sacred beauty of her oblation is consummated through her self-surrender as the prey of God. Without holding anything back, she wants God to devour her existence with His love. This is what it means to be the Host of Praise. The Host of Praise is the right and just response to the eucharistic sacrifice — the living context of this prayer, Christ's own prayer prayed in her. He offers Himself as food for us; we offer ourselves to the Trinity as prey. She means for her whole existence to be surrendered into the love of God. If God descends upon humanity as His prey, it is because Divine Eros has fashioned something so beautiful it is worthy of being devoured. When God devours, He never diminishes His handiwork but brings it to perfection.

The ravishing beauty that haunts St. Elizabeth's prayer has a mutual and reciprocal character. This mutuality and reciprocity echo the Mystery of the Holy Trinity, in the eternal relations of the Father, the Son, and the Holy Spirit. Just as this eternal glory is ravishing in God Himself, so too is the presence of the Holy Trinity in the prayer of the baptized. Authentic Christian contemplation is ecclesial because, caught up in the Trinity, the Bride of Christ beholds and is beheld by the Divine Persons of the Trinity in a unity of Light, Love, and Life.

St. Elizabeth does not simply see the form; she is seen by Him, and this enraptures her. He is also ravished by her. The deep hope and terror, the joy and sorrow, that swell in a bridegroom's heart as he beholds the radiance of his bride, remain only a faint hint of how a soul ablaze in love ravishes God. In a mysterious way, God permits love's terror to grip Christ as He beholds His bride-even-unto-death. Her death expresses her sacrificial love, a love given entirely, nothing withheld. St. Elizabeth thirsts to respond to this love *unto death* with her love. Her prayer culminates with a double burial: the entombment of God in the soul and of the soul in God. *Bury Yourself in me that I might bury myself in You.*

The Trinity initiates mutual surrender between God and the soul, but the soul attracts God through the grace of vulnerable surrender to His mystery. Theologians explain we may not ascribe any change to the Divine Nature, the One who St. Elizabeth calls "my Immutable." Yet she also speaks of God being drawn to the soul. This expresses a new kind of divine likeness achieved through the soul's participation in His life by grace. God is eternally drawn by His own perfections, and the highest work of grace in this life allows God to communicate these eternal perfections in the soul. This is called the grace of transforming union: through this grace, His own eternal perfections live in the frailty of humanity and He is drawn. Put differently, God is ravished in the sense that the soul transformed by grace and God both share mutually in this divine dynamism in the soul where each surrenders itself to the other. This love is drawn and drawing, ravished and ravishing, even devoured and devouring. Elizabeth expresses this mystery when she states that the Trinity "entombs" or "buries" Himself in our frailty, floods our whole existence with Himself. He buries Himself more deeply in His dwelling place, House of God. She "buries" herself in Him insofar as she lives no longer her own life, but His life in her, surrendered to Him to whom she belongs as His home.

Surrendering to the devouring love of the Trinity is not a prosaic wish but the finest moment of the human person before God. Anyone who has been ravished by beauty knows this terror. It promises joy and sorrow all at once; one feels as if he might explode. What grips the soul is too tremendous to be contained. This mystery of our final end must be that to which we humbly surrender or from which we tragically turn away. The last lines of St. Elizabeth's *Oblation to the Trinity* witness to the terrifying greatness of what she yearns to see.

These lines do not point to a single state of consciousness but to the beautiful cause of a fullness of conscious states until the surrender of the soul. God constantly generates this splendor anew, entirely consuming us as we consume Him. One encounters, all at once, the fullness of life and meaning. This unfolding, inexhaustible fullness is excessive for our whole being, including the eyes of our soul. Even when only the smallest portion of this fullness captures our consciousness, the divine inflow surpasses our soul's capacity. We are flooded, inundated, baptized, more or less aware of what is happening to us. Nothing of this divine self-disclosure is mastered, rather it masters us. We scratch only the surface of this mystery even after a lifetime. The splendor of the Beloved calls out to the depths of our being, evoking our response.

St. Elizabeth invites us into a very perilous encounter, into a place of utter vulnerability. A movement takes hold of the heart that we must sanction or we will be lost. The God who made Himself vulnerable on the Cross for us calls us into vulnerability with Him. He calls us with the love stronger than death to stand before Him so that He might receive our own frail, limited love. The failure to render what the beauty of another calls forth from our depths is to be diminished as a person. Yet, any attempt we make to respond, no matter how imperfect, places us on the very precipice of truth. This truly is a dangerous height upon which the mystery of one's heart is unveiled for all to see, with all the humiliation and glory such revelations must entail. This is a crisis, a moment of judgment. Here the Great Mystery in its baptismal and nuptial significance touches death. Faith sees the greatness of love most clearly at death; the hope of what it holds is only realized when it is buried. The ultimate horizon of the Eschaton lures us forward.

The *Catechism of the Catholic Church* wisely places Elizabeth's *Oblation* in the context of the ultimate end of the divine economy: the perfect unity of creatures with the Creator (*CCC* 260). Emmanuel, God with us, has made His home in the soul and in the world as House of God. This unity is presented not merely as a future event, but as a mystery already begun to be realized and known by faith, God being All in all.

If so, then contemplative prayer, as a simple movement of love, opens into a personal relationship that touches the ultimate purpose of human existence, and of the cosmos itself. The very structure of the world and the structure of the human heart are meant to flow with a beauty that comes from Another. St. Elizabeth sees this Splendor. She is captivated and caught up. Her heart is ravished by triune Beauty, and instead of holding on to it, she surrenders to it in a mutual indwelling with God All-Love.

CHAPTER TWO

Caught Up in the Trinity—Maybe It Is Not What We Would Expect

Then, through all nights, all voids, all weaknesses, I want always to gaze on You and to abide in Your great light.

FAITH ANTICIPATES THE FINAL fullness of union with God, yet faith is not yet sight. Through all *nights* I want to remain in Your light. Light in the night, the night as light; how can this be? Perhaps the words of St. Elizabeth of the Trinity in the opening stanza of her prayer to the Trinity, that I may be *established in You, still and peaceful, as if my soul were already in eternity*, do not mean what we might first imagine. Perhaps the apex of the spiritual life this side of the Eschaton may leave us bewildered. Being *established* in the Trinity, *still and peaceful* as if already in eternity, is probably not what we would expect. We are captivated and caught up, but caught up into what kind of movement?

A Soul That Is Pure Movement into the Trinity

The night as light: What is the quality of experience for those who *forget themselves in order to cleave to God by a wholly simple and loving movement*? This is how Elizabeth expresses it in describing her mission.

> *It seems to me that in Heaven, my mission will be to draw souls, helping them forget themselves in order to cleave to God through a very simple and loving movement and to hold them in this great interior silence that permits God to imprint in these souls His very self, to transform them into Himself.* (L 335)

Can souls drawn out of themselves have the same experience as those firmly established in their *I? By a very simple and loving movement,* these souls are pure movement *ad Deum, in Trinitatem,* going out of themselves toward God and into the Trinity, in a *very simple and loving movement* that is gentle and at rest. Souls captivated by triune Love are caught up in the same self-emptying kenotic love of the Trinity of the Cross. Caught up not just *out* of themselves but caught up *into* the Trinity, they exist solely for God as a praise of His glory — that *my life is nothing but a radiance of Your Life,* as Elizabeth puts it. Our self-giving love radiates the Trinity's self-giving Love as we turn from self to Him as a praise of glory, captivated and caught up ... and emptied out.

The first stanza of the prayer picks up the theme as well: help me to *forget myself entirely,* may each moment *carry me into the depths of Your Mystery*. Dynamically *carried* further into the *depths of mystery* with the self *forgotten* and left behind. How will this register in our ordinary knowing and loving? Perhaps as darkness. Perhaps as night, void, and helplessness. Maybe it would be better to keep busy with something more useful; anything to avoid facing this. Thus does our instinct for self-preservation urge us, *self*-preservation.

And the last stanza returns to the theme: *Immensity in whom I lose myself, I surrender myself to You as Your prey. Bury Yourself in me so that I may bury myself in You.* To *surrender* oneself entirely as the

Lord's prey and to be *buried* and hidden away also draws one out of a normal experience of self. The self must be hidden away in order to seek the Hidden One. Or better yet, it must be buried away in the One who has buried Himself in us, buried in the Beloved, the Other, who has lovingly buried Himself in us.

The triune God has buried Himself in us, through grace and the waters of Baptism, which begins our reciprocal being buried in Him. How can there be room for both in the soul? Surely the Trinity and the false self or the old man cannot both dwell in the same space. Will it be one's own glory or a Praise of God's glory? There's not room for both. *I surrender myself to You as Your prey* so the old man can be consumed. Then the wide-eyed, open child will remain, now re-born and full of wonderment over the mystery of God, truly captivated and so truly caught up.

Transcending Oneself in Love of the Other

Calm my soul; make it Your heaven, Your beloved dwelling and Your resting place.

Ah, there is peace after the combat with the old man. The soul is a Heaven where God rests in His beloved. And God calls the soul to rest, not in herself, but in Him, her Beloved. The soul finds rest and peace in God, but at times it is a peace the world cannot understand. The peace promised to us is a peace that *transcends* all our understanding. What is this peace promised *to us*, yet at the same time *transcending us*? It is a peace found not so much in us as in the Other:

O my beloved Christ, crucified by love, I desire to be a bride for Your heart, I desire to cover You with glory, I want to love You … unto death!

A bride of His heart also has Him at the center of her heart, covering Him in glory as she gives Him glory. That is her purpose and, as such, her center of gravity is in the Other. The Praise of Glory exists for the Other.

The mystery of Jesus, the Son, as a subsistent relation to the Father, manifests the most radical foundation and goal of self-transcendence. Caught up in the dynamic of self-emptying love, we are caught up in the self-giving love of the Trinity and exist solely as a praise of His glory. The Son receives all from the Father and returns all to Him in the ecstatic Love of the Holy Spirit. Each triune Person is a subsistent relation, a pure orientation-toward-the-others. The soul, then, living as a *very simple and loving movement* toward the other and the divine Other, and being *carried* further into the depths of the mystery of the Other, expands its capacity for communion with Father, Son, and Spirit.

The Three exist precisely as only oriented toward the Other in their eternal exchange of love (*CCC* 221). It is no mistake, then, that it is precisely God as Trinity to whom Elizabeth prays: *Help me to forget myself entirely; My Three ... in whom I lose myself.* Losing oneself in the Three is turning totally to the other, as Father, Son, and Spirit are turned even more totally to the Other in their complete self-giving love within the Trinity.

I No Longer Live, but Christ Lives in Me

Elizabeth's soul is radically oriented toward the Other. Her soul is pure movement toward and into the Other, in a very simple and loving movement. By implication, her humanity is now at the complete disposal of the Other. The French School of spirituality went far in this direction, analogously describing Christ's life in the Christian soul as another incarnation, as if the human self was no longer there, giving place to the Person of the Son instead. The merely human self has been lost through self-denial, and one's humanity finds a new life and a new existence in the Son, perfectly surrendered and attuned to the Word. Elizabeth echoes this but with no overstatement and with a perfect poise, praying to Jesus:

But I feel my weakness and I ask You to "clothe me with Yourself." Identify my soul with all the movements of Your soul. Overwhelm me, invade me, substitute Yourself for me, until my life is nothing but a radiance of Your Life.

What does it mean to give place to Jesus, so that this other Person indwells our being? It means what the Scriptures long ago declared, "always being given up for Jesus' sake, so that the life of Jesus may be manifested in our mortal flesh" (2 Cor. 4:11). Jesus will be manifested in us, that my life may be *but a radiance of Your life,* a praise of glory of God's perfection. At times, the new life expanding is felt more as a death, a death to the old man. "It is no longer I who live, but Christ who lives in me" (Gal. 2:20). And what does this mean for Christian experience? What does it mean about the experience Elizabeth describes as being *established in You, still and peaceful, as if my soul were already in eternity*?

Still and Peaceful in the Divine Beloved

To return to the opening lines of Elizabeth's prayer: to be *established* in the Trinity, *still* and *peaceful as if my soul were already in eternity,* may not be what we expect it to be, for it is not about *my* experience but about having a share in the whole mystery of Christ. And how different is experience, for a self who no longer lives but Christ lives in him, who no longer lives for himself but for God, who is no longer possessive but is possessed by God! Elizabeth offers her whole being, that *I may be for Him another humanity in whom He renews His whole Mystery.*

Being *established* in the Trinity *still* and *peaceful* can be equally true in the sorrowful mysteries of the Rosary as in the joyful. What is the peace that transcends all understanding, but this peace that endures even on the Cross? What is the stillness that sinks down to the foundations, but this still point that abides even on the Cross? The Cross stands firm while the world turns (*Stat Crux dum volvitur orbis*).

Even here, and maybe especially here, on the Cross, we are established in the peace and stillness, not of our own self, but of the Beloved. It is the prayer "that Christ may dwell in your hearts through faith that you, being rooted and grounded in love, may have power to comprehend with all the saints what is the breadth and length and height and depth, and to know the love of Christ which surpasses knowledge" (Eph. 3:17–19). It is through faith that every detail of our life can be embraced as a share in the mystery of Christ, who lived completely as that "very simple and loving movement" of love toward His neighbor and toward His Father. His food was to do the will of the Father and accomplish His work, whatever that entailed.

Enrapt in the Love of the Trinity

In doing the Father's will we find the true meaning of self-transcendence. Is it leaving the self and world behind for God? Is it a forgetfulness of all else but God? Is it an ecstatic silencing of self and being caught up in the abyss of God? Actually, yes, yes, and yes, to these questions. It should be like this at times. Communion with Father, Son, and Spirit is the highest good and is part of doing the will of the Father. This is what everything should tend toward. One is to be pitied for whom the infinite God is not enough. All else should be left behind, as we are, at times, caught up in the swirling love of the Trinity. This self-transcendence also involves living the other aspects of the life of Christ, the whole mystery of Christ, in His constant obedience to the will of the Father.

His self-giving love manifests itself in the ardor, strength, and tenderness of His service to His neighbor and also in His nights of silent prayer on the mountain, where the breeze circling up the mountainside carries a hint of triune enrapturement. We too manifest the triune self-giving love in these same movements, caught up in the triune life and radiating triune Love as a praise of glory. This movement involves the ecstasy of Christian service, living the life of Jesus, the man for others, and entering into self-forgetful service of others. Being a soul that is pure movement toward God and into the Trinity — *a very simple and loving movement* — means being a pure movement of love toward our neighbor as well. The neighbor we see carries us forward in self-forgetfulness into the mystery of the God we cannot see.

Living for the other also orients us to the divine Other. We are gathered together on the mountain with Jesus the Son as the breeze of the Holy Spirit spirals up the mountain to the Father, sweeping across the face of Jesus and our faces — neighbor to neighbor — sweeping through the breath of Jesus and our breath, bearing us upwards. And the Breeze and the God-Man come down into our lowest valleys, enwrapping everything and drawing it all up the mountain to the Father.

In sharing in the whole mystery of Christ, we are enraptured in the Trinity. "Enrapt" means most profoundly "enwrapped" in the Trinity. It is not just that we are on one side and God on the other, as we are graciously summoned to approach Him. More than this, God has stepped over fully and completely onto our side in the incarnate Son and draws us up with Him through the Spirit, in His return to the Father. Our ups and downs, our satisfactions and frustrations, our joys and sufferings, our consolations and desolations, and all our activities and states of mind and heart are enfolded within the trinitarian life. The Son and Spirit stand behind us and act within us in support and enrichment of our self-offering to the Father, for we are taken up into their very own offering to the Father. We are enfolded on all sides by triune Love.

The penultimate stanza of Elizabeth's prayer captures this image, as we are overshadowed by the cloud of the Spirit, under the loving gaze of the Father, and in the Beloved Son:

> *And You, O Father, bend down over Your poor little creature, see in her only the Beloved in whom You have placed Your delight.*

All is enwrapped in the triune mystery, even our nights, voids, and helplessness; so even these are turned into light by the obscure light of faith. And this overshadowing from God is the bright cloud of triune Love. The Praise of Glory manifests God's love in everything, as she lives for Him and not herself. Captivated by triune Love, she is caught up in triune Love and even her nights, voids, and helplessness radiate triune Love as she is being consumed.

CHAPTER THREE

Consumed—A Share in God's Thirst

Bridegroom and bride are so united that their hearts beat in unison, her heart echoing His. *O my beloved Christ, crucified by love, I desire to be a bride for Your Heart.* And it is Love, for St. Elizabeth, who is the author of her desire for God and for others. As the chosen beloved, the bride, loved with a singular love, St. Elizabeth draws into herself the very love that held Jesus to the Cross in expiation of our sins. Captivated and caught up, she begins to be consumed. In desiring to be made the bride of the Crucified, she is asking to be made the object of His love, a love which goes beyond all limits to Christ's very death. But she is also asking to be made more completely one with the Bridegroom's love in its yearning, even as He thirsts from the Cross.

St. Elizabeth wants spousal union with her Crucified Bridegroom. The bride is not only loved by the Bridegroom, she also makes His Sacrifice her own by participation. *Each seems to be the other and the two are but one* (LR 19). This Suffering Servant, the Son of God, mocked, scorned, and stripped, will be covered with glory by His bride who, totally stripped and set free of her self and all else, is compelled by her love to join with Him in loving ... even *unto death!* Which is, in fact, the one limit that cannot be avoided, but only defeated in Love's embrace. God's love is stronger than death.

This participation, a true sharing, can be entered into by such poor creatures as truly we are. At times our souls cry out: Love me completely; take me all! We see that deeper union, total union, means union with the Crucified. We long for crucifixion, if this is love's fullest surrender, yet we discover ourselves crippled by mediocrity and faults. St. Elizabeth knew this to be true of herself as well (LR 18). Yet she allowed Christ Himself to be her remedy. *I feel my weakness and I ask You to "clothe me with Yourself." Identify my soul with all the movements of Your soul.*

I LIVE, NO LONGER I, BUT CHRIST LIVES IN ME

Rather than turning away discouraged by her own incapacity to fulfill the great task of sharing in Christ's Passion, she found in her lack, weakness, and neediness a source of even deeper longing. Her love was strengthened by her increased desire. Urged on by her intensified thirst for love and her recognition of God's thirst for her, St. Elizabeth surrendered herself to her longing and begged God: *Overwhelm me, invade me, substitute Yourself for me, until my life is nothing but a radiance of Your Life.*

She allowed her desire for God to grow into an insatiable thirst. Not even more love was enough for her; she wanted to surrender herself completely to her Bridegroom to the point that He would live in her as *Adorer, Reparator, and Savior* more and more perfectly until she would finally penetrate into the interior of the Trinity to enjoy *the repose of the abyss* and become *the splendor of His glory* (LR 44). The House of God allowed the Lord to live in her more fully and, living His life, she existed as the splendor and praise of His glory. It is *so simple,* St. Elizabeth wrote, *the divine Adorer is within us, so we have His prayer; let us offer it, let us share in it, let us pray with His Soul!* (L 179).

As the bride of His Heart, she is particularly sensitive to His desire for our reciprocating love. She recognizes His longing for us as the origin of our longing for Him, for His love. The thirst which eventually consumes her as a host of praise echoes God's own thirst; this intensifies her thirst. St. Elizabeth wills to be perfectly and completely conformed to the Crucified and His work of salvation through His power at work in her. To do the will of the Father, to receive and believe in His love, is the *nourishment* of the bride because this is what *nourishes the bridegroom,* and, moreover, just as it was for the Bridegroom, the will of the Father is also *the sword that pierces her* until she rejoices *to "have been known" by the Father since He is crucifying her with His Son* (LR 38).

Still she thirsts. In her surrender, she discovers that God's quenching of our thirst portends a consequent increase in thirst until love's final consummation in Heaven, until the soul has *become holy with His holiness* (LR 29). Her entire oblation is a crescendo of thirst, loving surrender, increased thirst, and greater entrustment of herself. This movement is not simply for her own satisfaction, it is driven by her desire to glorify God as His praise of glory. Her growing intimacy with her Bridegroom is precisely a deeper union with the Divine Adorer, *He who is the great praise of glory to the Father* (LR 38).

For Elizabeth, adoration is being captivated and caught up to the point of self-forgetfulness. She calls this *ecstasy of love* and defines it as *Love shattered by the beauty, the power, the immense grandeur of the Object loved ... it "falls prostrate, overwhelmed" before a profound, total silence, that silence of which David spoke when he exclaimed: "Silence is your praise!" Yes, this is the loveliest praise. Eternally chanted in the bosom of the peaceful Trinity, a soul's final push abounds into speechlessness* (LR 21).

The beauty, power, and grandeur of the Trinity shatter love's limits until the soul prostrates itself in profound silence. This loving silence shares in the praise that lives in the heart of the Trinity. For the sake of this love, and that we might share it with her, St. Elizabeth urges us to join her in offering ourselves to be consumed, like the Virgin, to silently *adore with Jesus the will of God, who wounds solely because He loves* (L 142).

Great love wounds self-satisfaction. True love is neither comfortable nor convenient but demanding. And precisely in the difficult sacrifices that love demands we discover the truth about ourselves. The Father wants to associate us with Christ's work of redemption, Love's greatest work of all. *Mary learned from the Word Himself how those whom the Father has chosen as victims must suffer. These are those whom He has resolved to associate with Himself in His great work of redemption. These are they He "has foreknown and predestined to be conformed to His Christ," being crucified by love.* (LR 41).

Addressing herself to the *Eternal Word, Word of my God,* she begs to spend her life *listening,* to *become completely docile, in order to learn everything from [Him]*. St. Elizabeth knows this Word, spoken by the Father, spoken into her own heart at her Baptism, as a loving longing for Him alone. She longs to consume and to be consumed. *Bury Yourself in me so that I may bury myself in You.*

The Word in her attracts the love of the Holy Spirit, and herein lies the increase in her thirst, her longing, her desire for more Love. Her reply is deeper, most trusting surrender, in order to receive more — not just more, but All! — from her Three, All-Love, until she is *like another incarnation of the Word, that I may be for Him another humanity in whom He renews His whole Mystery,* until she is buried, as she was first in Baptism, now fully in her *Three,* as the Three are also buried in her, Elizabeth, House of God.

Having forgotten herself entirely and gone out from herself, as a pure praise of God's glory, St. Elizabeth braves all her *nights, voids, and weaknesses.* She anchors her gaze on God in His *great light,* praying to be so fascinated *that I cannot leave your splendor.* Then she can cover Him in glory. In gazing, St. Elizabeth receives from the Crucified His own gaze of love from the Cross, as He searches out any who would surrender themselves to Love in order to receive and be made one with His Oblation, His total self-Sacrifice, His own perfect surrender to the Father's will for the salvation of the world and the redemption of all creation. He searches out those who would quench His thirst for love by *letting themselves be loved* (L 337).

Standing by the Cross … "Jesus saw his mother, and the disciple whom he loved standing near … After this Jesus, knowing that all was now finished, said (to fulfil the scripture), 'I thirst'" (John 19:26, 28). It is the Mother and the Beloved Disciple here on Calvary for whom the Praise of Glory is an icon.

> *A praise of glory is a soul fixed on God in faith and simplicity … A soul which thus allows the divine Being to satiate within it his need to communicate "all that He is and all that He has" is truly a praise of glory of all his gifts.*
>
> …
>
> *Finally, a praise of glory is a being in perpetual thanksgiving. Each of its acts, its movements, its thoughts, its aspirations, at the same time as they are rooted more radically in love, echo the eternal* Sanctus. *(HF 43)*

As Christ the Crucified Bridegroom, gazing down on Mary and John from the height of the Cross, because of His great love for us allowed our sins to wound Him, St. Elizabeth too tastes the sweetest intimacy with Him by sharing in His act of reckless love for souls. Driven by her thirst to quench His thirst for our love, she receives His gaze, seeking ever-deepening intimacy and allowing herself to be joined to Him in

His work of reparation: *O consuming Fire, Spirit of Love, spread in me until my soul is filled, like another incarnation of the Word, that I may be for Him another humanity in whom He renews His whole Mystery.*

She holds nothing back because until she tastes fully of the Lord, she will not be fully offered to Him. Long has she known that God was dwelling in her, but her now-wild thirst, her consuming desire for her Crucified Bridegroom, will, as her life draws to its end, lead her to beg to be made a host of praise, Love's victim. She is no longer simply House of God, nor even *Laudem Gloriae* (Praise of Glory), gazing on God and reflecting Him, which was her vocation-within-a-vocation and which she lived to the heights of sanctity. She wants more. Her thirst drives her to drink to the dregs.

Total identification with her Bridegroom, even in His Sacred Victimhood, to be another humanity in which the Word has His whole mystery renewed, and nothing less, is her desire. *To be an extra-added humanity for Him in which He can extend His life of reparation, sacrifice, praise, and adoration. Ask Him that I may fulfil my vocation and not waste the graces He lavishes on me ... I entrust myself to Him, "the Faithful and True," as St. John says, and I beg Him to be my fidelity!* (L 256).

This thirst that we share, most often in small and nearly imperceptible ways, is our invitation to greater surrender and, consequently, increased thirst. We too are God's beloved, in whom He is well-pleased, when we lovingly gaze upon Him to receive His gaze of self-giving Love. With St. Elizabeth, we can have a role in quenching God's thirst for our love — by receiving Him, surrendering ourselves to Him, allowing His love to be incarnated in our lives through our *Quotidie morior*, the daily death to self, and by receiving and believing in His love for us. The Word will then adore, will make reparation, and will save — in us and through us.

The surrender required is radical; such intimate love requires nothing less than everything. Ultimately, St. Elizabeth makes herself God's *prey* — hunted, captured, and devoured. She must hold back nothing of herself; she will be consumed. Her thirst will be satisfied only in the total loss necessary to quench God's thirst for her love. Our thirst can imitate hers.

St. Elizabeth's insatiable longing for Love, first given to her in Baptism, did bring her to offer herself entirely: *If I raise the cup reddened with the Blood of my Maestro . . . I mingle my blood with the Blood of the holy Victim* (LR 18). She truly became another humanity for God. *We must be transformed into Jesus Christ* (LR 37), she wrote — echoing St. Paul — so that God's will might be accomplished in us and we might come to share in the very communion of the Trinity (LR 43), thanks to God's insatiable thirst for our love and in Love's total self-gift. With her Crucified Bridegroom *she drinks the last bitter drop of "the chalice the Father has prepared"; she tastes divine sweetness* (LR 39).

Her thirst and Christ's thirst come together in the sharing of this cup. The suffering is not indefinite. The evil that the work of redemption bears away eventually exhausts itself against God's love, and in the end love remains. Her thirst to possess Him in glory will be consummated in her final surrender. *Finally, after saying so often "I thirst," a thirst to possess You in glory, she sings: "It is finished: into Your hands I commend my spirit." And the Father will come "to share His inheritance with her" where in "light she will see light"* (LR 39).

CONCLUSION

DRAWN BY GOD

SEEN IN ITS PROPER context, we do not pray St. Elizabeth's *Oblation to the Trinity* merely as a heroic act of virtue or an exertion of our love. Rather, we make the offering as a response to the gift of God. When we pray the *Oblation to the Trinity*, we already are being held and lifted up by Father, Son, and Holy Spirit as we share in the triune Life. We offer ourselves entirely to the Trinity while already buoyed up on the Ocean of Love in the Father, Son, and Holy Spirit.

The Trinity draws and fascinates us. We are captivated. We are almost mesmerized by the beauty of God as we pursue the main purpose of life, the One Thing Necessary. Seeking the face of the Beloved in everything becomes our life's wholesome obsession. Enthralled by God's beauty, we grow wings in our ascent to God.

The Trinity draws us beyond ourselves and lifts us. We are caught up. As we set our hearts on heavenly things, we bear the scent of Heaven amidst our life on earth (see Col. 3:1–4). As we desire God and the things of God we are brought beyond our petty selfish desires. Old ways are left behind as we take up our place in the new creation in Jesus Christ (see 2 Cor. 5:17). Self-forgetfulness ultimately comes not so much by working harder at forgetting self but by being captivated and caught up beyond ourselves to God.

The Trinity draws us and pours us out in our self-offering of love. We are consumed. Acts of self-denial and self-giving love are required, but much more takes place beyond what we initiate. We offer ourselves, but find on a deeper level that we ourselves are being offered. We accept this with our *fiat* to God and His ways in our lives and, as a result, we are poured out by Him. God thirsts for us. He thirsts for our thirst of love for Him, and He is intent on bringing about this free offering of love as we are poured out.

The Trinity draws us by grace, and we experience this as a fascination with God's beauty, as we are lifted up beyond our self to the things of God and poured out in our self-offering to the Blessed Trinity. Captivated, we know God more intimately as we gaze upon His charming mystery. Caught up, we desire things above as we are drawn to God more than self. Consumed, our *fiat* of the obedience of faith gives all to God and allows all to be taken. Captivated, caught up, and consumed, we are offered to God as He draws us to Himself.

Named for Mutual Belonging

O my Three, my All, my Beatitude, infinite Solitude, Immensity in whom I lose myself, I surrender myself to You as Your prey. Bury Yourself in me so that I may bury myself in You, while waiting to go contemplate in Your light the abyss of Your grandeurs.

It is the transcendent, infinite Most High God to whom St. Elizabeth says, "My Three, my All." The personal intimacy of that *My* is staggering even in its delicacy. The Three have given themselves to her so she can say, *My Three, my All*. Elizabeth has given herself entirely to the Three so she can say, *My Three, my All*. Surrendering herself not just as a prey of God but as *Your prey* captures this total giving over of herself to the Three in trust. Even if it feels like she is torn to pieces, everything collapses, and she is consumed, she surrenders herself in complete and radical trust as *your prey*. She belongs entirely to the Three in personal intimate love. She loses herself not as if annihilated before the Infinite but rather in love of her Three as *Your prey*. *My Three, my All*.

For Elizabeth, *My Three, my All* is the *Immensity in whom I lose myself*— and this, only to find herself in God, now made new. She leaves the old names behind — me, myself, and I — for the *Immensity in whom I lose myself*. She leaves the old names behind to find herself in God, now as House of God, Praise of Glory, and Host of Praise. For there is another part to her thought here: *Bury Yourself in me so that I may bury myself in You*. Here is a mutuality that expresses the Divine Indwelling of Persons. The triune God buries Himself in Elizabeth as House of God, Praise of Glory, and Host of Praise, in Divine Indwelling, divine radiance, and divine consummation.

Persons are called by names, and new persons are called by new names. Lovers call out their beloved's name. *House of God, Praise of Glory, Host of Praise! My Three, my All!* In the beginning, Mary's lifelong *fiat* opened the path of this new creation that Elizabeth trod with her new names, and this path remains wide open for us as we, strengthened by their company, now cry out, *My Three, my All!*

Named and Claimed by God's Love

The triune God of Love has a loving plan for each one of us, and this plan situates us in our place among others in a communion of love. Father, Son, and Holy Spirit go before us in the accomplishment of this beautiful purpose of our life, leading us to the communion of love. God has named us as His own and has gifted us with a share in His own life through grace. St. Elizabeth's names as House of God, Praise of Glory, and Host of Praise helped her find her place in God's plan in this world and in eternity.

How do we view disappointment? How about affliction and suffering? Is it a case of bad luck? Or getting what we deserve? Or is it part of an unfolding plan that is larger than we are and guided by a wisdom of love that is loftier than our limited ideas? St. Elizabeth of the Trinity saw the misfortunes of life as part of her love story with the Divine Maestro. They fit within her canticle of love and intensified her thirst. Elizabeth as Host of Praise or Victim of Praise accepted these sufferings from the hand of the Father, like Jesus, the Beloved Son Himself, did. As Host of Praise, she found meaning in her afflictions, by which she shared in the cruel death of her Crucified Bridegroom, now offered to the Father in love and for the salvation of souls.

How about us? How do we view opportunities in life? Are they just a chance to get ahead, to accomplish something to our credit and make something of ourselves? Or are they primarily opportunities to glorify God with our gifts and talents — or maybe even glorify God through our lackluster performance and faltering efforts, yet carried out as a canticle of love? St. Elizabeth lived as a praise of glory. This was who she was, and it allowed her to turn everything into an opportunity to glorify God. Her whole life and being was unto the praise of God's glorious grace returned to the Father in thankful praise.

How do we view our relationships? Are they just a way to avoid our loneliness, to receive some emotional gratification and consolation from others? Or are our relationships about a genuine communion of self-giving love built on the God who is Love? St. Elizabeth, as House of God, had communion at the center of her life, communion with the indwelling Trinity and with others. Hers was not the solitude of loneliness but of dwelling with the One Thing Necessary, the Three Persons Necessary. And enfolded within this Love of the Trinity, she dwelt with others in the Communion of Love.

House of God, Praise of Glory, and Host of Praise also mark our identity in Christ. We were gifted with these names in our Baptism, and we grow in this identity as we grow in grace. We are not employing a self-help tactic or a self-initiated exertion of willpower; we are responding to a gift received. St. Elizabeth received these names from God as a gift. God's gracious gift is the fundamental factor.

God's eternal designs of love have named us for glory. The gift of our identity in Christ is given a fuller expression in the names House of God, Praise of Glory, and Host of Praise. These God-gifted names open up before us the dimensions of our life in Christ and our dwelling in communion with the Blessed Trinity and all the saints. Elizabeth has opened up vistas for us in delving into this mystery.

We have journeyed with St. Elizabeth of the Trinity, drawing insights from her about the life of grace through the prism of these three names, House of God, Praise of Glory, and Host of Praise. In part 1, we saw how Mary, Gate of Heaven, is a gateway for Elizabeth into the rich contours of these three names and how Mary's *fiat* informs our own response to this gift of grace. In part 2, we saw how the eternal designs of God surrounding our identity as House of God, Praise of Glory, and Host of Praise exert their effect in our spiritual life. In part 3, we considered Elizabeth's *Oblation to the Trinity* as the activity that follows from this identity; the soul is captivated, caught up, and consumed by triune Love. St. Elizabeth calls us to make a radical shift from self to God, so the primary name that remains on our lips is *My Three, My All!*

ABOUT THE AUTHORS

FR. IGNATIUS JOHN SCHWEITZER, O.P., is a Dominican priest of the St. Joseph (Eastern) Province. He was ordained in 2011 and spent six years living as a monk in a Carthusian monastery, entering into great silence with St. Elizabeth. He then returned to the Dominicans, discerning a strong call from the Lord to help others grow in the spiritual and mystical life. Upon returning, he completed his S.T.L., writing on "The Life, Light, and Fire of Triune Love: A Trinitarian Spirituality from Scripture, Aquinas, Ruusbroec, and John of the Cross." He is the promoter of the Dominican Laity, professor, spiritual director, and Director of Spiritual Formation at St. Joseph's Seminary. He has a YouTube channel: Dominican House of Prayer. It has many videos on the spiritual life. He also has a website www.UpperGarden.org, with essays on the spiritual life. He hopes to be of service to the Lord's loving cry to souls and souls' cry to the Lord: "Abyss calls to abyss!"

JULIE ENZLER IS A devoted wife, mother, and grandmother who discovered St. Elizabeth of the Trinity as a student at Franciscan University and has made her more widely known through courses and the careful translation of Sr. Giovanna della Croce's *Elizabeth of the Trinity: A Life of Praise to God* for Sophia Institute Press. She holds a licentiate in sacred theology from the Pontifical University of St. Thomas, a B.A. in theology and philosophy from Franciscan

University of Steubenville, and formation certificates for all levels of Catechesis of the Good Shepherd. She has worked as a teacher and a catechist and as a translator for *L'Osservatore Romano,* and she founded New England Classical Academy, a K–12 classical curriculum academy in the Catholic tradition.

PROFESSOR ANTHONY LILLES IS a husband and father who provides retreats, blog posts, and podcasts on St. Elizabeth of the Trinity's spiritual mission around the world. Professor Lilles has taught graduate-level theology since 1994, having served at St. Thomas Aquinas Seminary in Denver, St. John Vianney Theological Seminary in Denver, and St. John's Seminary in Camarillo prior to joining the faculty of St. Patrick's Seminary. With a B.A. in theology from Franciscan University of Steubenville, as well as an ecclesiastical licentiate and doctorate in spiritual theology from the Pontifical University of St. Thomas, he has specialized in St. Elizabeth of the Trinity and the Carmelite Doctors of the Church. He co-founded the Avila Institute for Spiritual Formation and the High Calling Program for priestly vocations. He also founded and serves as president of the John Paul II Center for Contemplative Culture. His work at St. Patrick's began in 2014 when he helped start an annual summer spirituality program. He was appointed Academic Dean from 2019 to 2022 before joining the full-time teaching and formation faculties. From 2024 through 2027, he will be committed to a new Initiative for Priestly Renewal jointly sponsored by St. Patrick's Seminary and the High Calling program of the Avila Foundation. He blogs at Spiritual Direction and podcasts at Discerning Hearts. In October 2024, Dr. Lilles launched *Spiritual Revolution: A Journal of Mystical Theology* on Substack.

Sophia Institute

Sophia Institute is a nonprofit institution that seeks to nurture the spiritual, moral, and cultural life of souls and to spread the gospel of Christ in conformity with the authentic teachings of the Roman Catholic Church.

Sophia Institute Press fulfills this mission by offering translations, reprints, and new publications that afford readers a rich source of the enduring wisdom of mankind.

Sophia Institute also operates the popular online resource CatholicExchange.com. *Catholic Exchange* provides world news from a Catholic perspective as well as daily devotionals and articles that will help readers to grow in holiness and live a life consistent with the teachings of the Church.

In 2013, Sophia Institute launched Sophia Institute for Teachers to renew and rebuild Catholic culture through service to Catholic education. With the goal of nurturing the spiritual, moral, and cultural life of souls, and an abiding respect for the role and work of teachers, we strive to provide materials and programs that are at once enlightening to the mind and ennobling to the heart; faithful and complete, as well as useful and practical.

Sophia Institute gratefully recognizes the Solidarity Association for preserving and encouraging the growth of our apostolate over the course of many years. Without their generous and timely support, this book would not be in your hands.

www.SophiaInstitute.com
www.CatholicExchange.com
www.SophiaTeachers.org

Sophia Institute Press is a registered trademark of Sophia Institute.
Sophia Institute is a tax-exempt institution as defined by the
Internal Revenue Code, Section 501(c)(3). Tax ID 22-2548708.